a loving home

a loving home

spirituality, sexuality, and healing black life

Lee H. Butler Jr.

FORTRESS PRESS
MINNEAPOLIS

A LOVING HOME
Spirituality, Sexuality, and Healing Black Life

Fortress Press ex libris publication 2007

Cover design: Martha A. Clark
Cover photo © Elma Garcia/Photonica/Getty Images.
Used by permission.

ISBN-13: 978-0-8006-6267-7

The Library of Congress has catalogued the original publication as follows:

Library of Congress Cataloging-in-Publication Data
Butler, Lee H.,   1959-
A loving home: spirituality, sexuality, and healing black life.
Includes bibliographical references.
ISBN: 0-8298-1395-0
1. Interpersonal relations—Religious aspects—Christianity. 2. African Americans—Religion. 3. African Americans—Kinship. 4. Sex—Religious aspects—Christianity. I. Title.
BV4597.52 .B88 2000
306.81'089'96073—dc21

Manufactured in the U.S.A.

*To everyone who has prayed for me
and encouraged me on this journey*

Contents

Foreword

This is an important book, and as with any book it has an intended audience. That audience includes primarily African Americans who are concerned with the vitality of African American couples and families, as well as anyone who works with African American couples and families in a pastoral or counseling relationship. In addition, teachers at either the college, graduate, or seminary level will gain tremendous insight into African American culture and families, and this book will be a "must" on any syllabus seeking to be inclusive and cross-cultural.

African American readers will be taken on a journey home, historically, spiritually, and psychologically. I have just returned from my second journey to Ghana, West Africa. For me, this journey is a pilgrimage—a journey home—for it is there that I find my connection to my true self and my ancestors, my peace and my place. When one journeys to Ghana, one is confronted with the origins of the European-driven slave industry, symbolized by the dungeons of Elmina and Cape Coast, which Lee Butler so vividly describes in chapter 3. Each time I have made the pilgrimage to these dungeons, as I stood there where my foremothers stood, one of the things I heard, almost audibly above my own inaudible screams, were the screams of the *men,* held in these dungeons only feet away, who could not rescue me. These men, some kings or princes or warriors, could not protect or help their sisters. Each time I stood there, what came to me as tears ran down my face was the realization that this is probably where the difficulties in our collective relational history between African American women and men began. What stands between us? A walking tour of Cape Coast and Elmina dungeons gives us our first indications.

My brother in scholarship and struggle Lee Butler has heard these same screams and laments as he has penned these pages. He and I have lectured together on the emergence of Womanist-care and pastoral care for African American men. We have each researched and written about the yearnings of African American men and women to find our way back home to one another. Our history of the dungeons, the Middle Passage, chattel slavery, and Jim Crow has caused us to become separated from our bodies, ourselves, our sexuality, our spirituality, and one another. This separation manifests itself in contemporary times in many ways; as "hide and go seek," isolation, mistrust, communication difficulties, infidelity, and lack of relational commitment. This separation has hurt us individually and collectively.

Lee Butler sends out a clarion call for us to come home. He sees our African understandings of God and humanity as foundational to our fully embracing who we are as an African (American) people—as the whole people of God. We are a communal people and cannot find our individual selves without fully embracing our fundamental *inter*dependence, for truly, as the Akan proverb states: "I am because we are, and because we are, therefore I am." This understanding is in direct contrast to the Western/Jungian concept of individuation, wherein the person moves from community (family) to stand *apart* in order to become fully autonomous. In the African cognizance, while one may move outside of community to perform rituals or rites of passage, one has not fully completed these rites until one has *returned* to and been reincorporated into the community.

As I shopped in the craft villages of Ghana, I was drawn to a particular wood carving of a person climbing a tree with one (or two, depending on the carving) people under him or her, pushing him or her up. I asked, "What does this carving mean?" I was told that it is the representation of an Akan proverb: *Wo foro dua pa a ena wo pia wo.* "When you climb a good tree then you will get support"; or "When you do something with good intentions someone will help you." For Africans, this is another way of indicating the centrality of interconnectedness. One cannot work well in isolation; one must have the support and assistance of the community—we must pull together for progress to take place. For me, and hopefully for you, this book and the work of Lee Butler are another manifestation of this proverb. The journey toward home and wholeness is underway, and I am pledged to walk the path toward home with Lee and others, and to do my part to make it so.

MARSHA FOSTER BOYD
Director, Accreditation and Leadership Education
The Association of Theological Schools

Preface

This book represents my reflections upon all of my relationships. All that I am and hope to become is connected to everyone that I have encountered along the way. I owe a great debt of gratitude to everyone who has ever touched my life, beginning with the first Ancestor, God Almighty. This book is the articulation of many voices that became one voice. The generations of the known and unknown spoke to me day and night. They reviewed an African American spiritual history that is as close to us as our breath, and often just as invisible to us.

I thank my family, both near and far, for embodying the traditions of African and African American spirituality and Christian love. When my confidence was failing, the unwavering support of my family and friends sustained me. Many of them read these pages at different stages in the process. Their encouragement and feedback have been invaluable: my wife, Mary Anita Robinson Butler, who helps me to live and love; my mother, Geraldine G. Butler; my father, Lee H. Butler Sr. (deceased); my father-in-law, Edward Barnett; my grandparents, James (deceased) and Helen A. Green, Henry and Lurline Butler; my mother-in-law, Maureane Robinson; my great-aunt and great-uncle, Bernice and Elijah Davis (godparents); Arlen Vernava, Eric Branch, Cheryl Kirk-Duggan, JoAnne M. Terrell, Tammy Bell, Kathleen Greider, Peggy Kay, and the Paladino family.

My thanks for the inspiration and support of African and African American friends, families, and churches: Wade Nobles and Na'im Akbar, who served as mentors and guides through Ghana, West Africa; my Zulu family, the Mtetwas (Sipho, Xoli, Sine, Ndu, and Khethelo), who taught me the meaning of family adoption; Kathleen Coleman (deceased),

Dr. Mkhize, Arthur Pressley, Carroll Watkins Ali, Linda Parrish; Carla Tatum, Deborah Davis, and Sarah Davis Brazier, cousins who have been like sisters; aunts, uncles, and cousins; Third Baptist Church, Chicago; First Baptist Church, Steelton, Pennsylvania; Bethany Baptist Church, Newark, New Jersey; Mt. Calvary Baptist Church, Ardmore, Pennsylvania; Tabernacle Baptist Church, Harrisburg, Pennsylvania; Upper Room Baptist Church, Philadelphia; and the mighty cloud of ministerial witnesses.

Special thanks go to the ACTS pastoral theologians working group, the Society for the Study of Black Religion, the Chicago Theological Seminary family (the board, the administration, my colleagues, the staff, and the students), and my many godchildren.

Chapter 1

Living Whole and Holy Lives

Glorify God in your body, and in your spirit,
which are God's.

— I CORINTHIANS 6:20B (KJV)

This book asks you to examine yourself and your relationships. Through self-exploration, reflection, and questions to promote conversation, you will be encouraged to reconstruct your relational life. We will focus on the most significant relationships of African American life. Although you will be asked to consider spirituality and sexuality as the primary influences upon our relationships, you will also be asked to examine the relationships you have with God, yourself, your spouse, family, friends, and community.

REUNITING A SPLIT

Life is most fulfilling when it is lived out relationally. Spirituality purports to unify all things, yet our Western practices have split our spiritual functioning into the sacred and the profane, the spiritual and the mundane. This also applies to our understanding of sexuality in relation to spirituality. The splitting of the two has meant the splitting of our lives. Rather than spirituality and sexuality being unified to overcome human isolation, we have come to understand spirituality as the mortification of the body. The death of the body has also meant the condemnation of sexuality. The body has taken on the description of everything evil, with the citation that no good can come from the flesh.

1

This splitting of spirituality and sexuality has had a devastating impact upon African American relationships. African
Americans have been regarded as being without religion, spirit,
or morality—that is, without spirituality. Those who have
viewed the African with contempt have thought our nature
to be lustful, sensual, and animal, that is, uncontrolled sexuality. Historically, we have been seen as less than human and
therefore not spiritual. While some of us have believed these
outsiders' opinions, all of us have been influenced by these
opinions whether we believe them or not. Such opinions have
affected the ways we relate to one another. As a result, the splitting of the two has had a negative influence upon our relational
openness and intimacy.

SEEKING EQUALITY IN RELATIONSHIPS

As African American men and women in relationship with one
another, we find ourselves in a peculiar and precarious condition. We live during a time that says affirmative action is no
longer necessary. The work ethic has been revitalized to label
poverty the result of laziness. Both affirmative action and the
work ethic combine to say that America believes in fair play
and a level playing field. There is something terribly wrong with
this picture of equal opportunity. Our memory of "separate
and unequal" is too powerful to accept such a picture without examination. Inequality still looms large in our everyday
lives. Even with the equal opportunity picture, African Americans continue to be regarded by many as inferior and as people
who should be separated in the name of preserving America's
heritage.

Spirituality and sexuality are also seen as separate and unequal. Spirituality is seen as superior and sexuality as inferior.
Just as the work ethic is used to label poverty a result of
laziness, the most prominent spiritual ideas associate spiritual
poverty with expressions of sexuality. The poor in spirit are
thought to be those who are the most sensual. We have been
seduced into believing that our "holy dance" is always up and

down, never side to side. We have denied our humanity by separating our spiritual lives from our physical lives.

In this era of spiritual seekers searching for spiritual direction and new ways to understand spirituality, it is extremely important that African American perspectives and approaches guide the conversation for African Americans. Our lives have been influenced by less than helpful interpretations of spirituality and sexuality. We take great pride in declaring that we do not make separations, but the fact is, we separate many aspects of our lives. The separation of spirituality and sexuality is no exception. It is imperative that we end this mind-body split that we experience through the splitting of spirituality and sexuality. We must re-create our relationships.

Although some practical suggestions are offered, this book is not a how-to book; we have too many books of that type already. Of course many step-by-step manuals dish out great advice on how to make a marriage successful, more fun, or romantic. But deep relationships require more than the individualistic gaze at marriage alone. I interpret relational behaviors because insight into the things people do brings the power of change.

My intended readers are African Americans. But my pastoral counseling experience confirms that these insights can prove helpful for persons of many cultures. Indeed, my hope is that the psychospiritual insights offered here will better all the relationships of every African American. Our most significant relationships are explored to disclose the reasons we do the things that we do to one another. Examining what prompts us to think about one another in the ways we do will help us to become more than we are. Many African Americans are lost because we do not know ourselves fully as people in relationships. We can only improve the quality of our lives when we understand that we are who we are in community.

STEPS IN CARING

We have been socialized as men and women to be unequal players in relationship. Rather than giving one another full support, we support each other selectively. The basic goal for our relationships is to become equal partners concerned and committed to one another in an open and trusting way. Until we are able to become more supportive, we will continue to hurt one another. This means moving beyond the old stereotypical roles. It is important that we develop a different understanding of what is means to be in relationship as African Americans. Throughout this book, the things we have believed about ourselves are described. After each description you will be introduced to an alternative view of the issues.

Another basic goal is to initiate our re-creation through unifying spirituality and sexuality. We need new ways of understanding old ideas. Our redemption as a community rests in our ability to see that our behaviors in one area of life affect other areas of our lives. For all our relationships to be more fulfilling, we need to name the forces that split us apart. We live surrounded by the dividing lines of color, sex, gender, and class. Many of us have forsaken our communal identity as an American people of African descent. We have experienced difference as an enemy called "other." America has frequently regarded African Americans as "other." The nation's racism and sexism have identified us as the evil, black male and female. Our black body has been described as the unholy, unclean incarnation of evil in America. This description has had a damaging affect upon our relationships. Contrary to how we have been seen, our bodies are good, holy, and clean; African American relationships are not beyond repair. We can no longer afford to sacrificially escape our bodies by overspiritualizing our minds.

A third basic goal is to unify all our relationships. The individual, family, and community are always connected. They are not separate, unrelated parts. We are in need of healing to restore our humanity and our extended family. This book proposes new directions that will restore psychospiritual health and wholeness to our community. We need new ways to think about the quality of *all* our relationships. We need to be liberated and healed. *Liberation* is the transformation to freedom, power, and authority. *Healing* is necessary for establishing a new foundation for relating. The starting point is for us to begin to rethink the function of African American spirituality and sexuality.

Chapter 2 considers a few ideas related to growing into our relationships. Life begins relationally with two becoming one in the birth process. Fertilization is two, the egg and the sperm, becoming one. The *in utero* experience is a process of two, mother and child, living as one. The birth experience, then, becomes the first separation that every human being struggles to bridge. We all want our two-ness to become one again. Because we cannot simply return to the womb, we struggle to learn new ways of relating with the hope of finding contentment. This chapter presents some of the influential social and cultural conditions that affect and influence our basic understandings of relationship. I also briefly examine how openness and trust influence the quality of our relationships.

Chapter 3 explores the foundational dynamics of all our relationships as African American men and women. "Home" is explored as a metaphor in history and biblical narrative that suggests what we expect from one another in our relationships as friends, co-workers, family members, and suitors. The circumstances of our condition as African Americans and the issues involved in improving our relationships are presented. Our relational problems are shown as having their roots deep within our past as a people. I show the intricacies of racism's and sexism's impact upon our being and how these oppressions influence our behaviors. After describing our painful past, I point to possibilities for our healing and restoration. This chapter identifies the issues for the chapters that follow.

Chapter 4 focuses upon the traditional value system of community as a key component of African spirituality. Our relationships can be liberated and saved through the revival of our spiritual heritage. African spirituality is regularly highlighted as an African American saving grace, yet the ways in which it seems to be expressed in our contemporary context promote separation and otherness rather than unity. That is,

most are familiar with the thesis statement of African identity
and community: I am because we are, and because we are I am.
We say these words with such authority. But we no longer live
by the principle of communality.
Communality means that all people and things are inter-
related. African spirituality declares there are no separations.
Our combined relationships with the Divine, extended family, spouse, siblings, neighbors, private and public worship all
constitute communality. Today we are experiencing communal dysfunction because we have separated the church from
the community. Think about the instances when the church is
considered "out of touch" with the community. The church
members are thought to be "in" the community but not part
"of" the community. Chapter 4 explores the necessity of reuniting religiosity and community as the prerequisite for restoring
all of our relationships.

Chapter 5 revisits the Abraham, Sarah, Hagar, Ishmael, and
Isaac narrative developed in chapter 3 with an analysis of family structure and leadership. Our most basic system of support
and survival is the family. Unfortunately, there has been a decay
of the extended family system. African Americans have survived because the extended family taught us that responsibility
and interdependency are the power of relationships. One sign
of this decay is how many families have shifted from our extended family heritage to a focus on a nuclear family. In a time
when we were denied the security of family ties, our extended
family structure, which included blood and nonblood relations,
resisted social disintegration and fought against nonexistence.
We took responsibility for one another's well-being. Now we
are becoming more individualized and separating ourselves
from our traditional ideas of family.

Chapter 6 further explains our relational difficulties through
a focused exploration of evil and what it means to be men
and women in relationship with one another. All too often,
we confront evil through the oppressive processes of declaring difference or "otherness." The easiest way for people to
fight evil is to be able to point at it and say, "There it is."
Those who identify it commonly understand themselves to

be good. The other who has been identified as evil must be destroyed.

This chapter explores our relational practices of identifying men and women as evil to be controlled and destroyed. There is, however, an impulse that encourages us to unite with otherness despite our desires to destroy otherness. This is the reason why we say things like, "Men [or women], you can't live with them; you can't live without them." Although we continue to unite with those declared to be other, our efforts frequently are deceptive and destructive. Before we can transform these behaviors, our self-understanding needs to be renewed. Here the emphasis is upon renewing our understandings of manhood, of womanhood, and of what it means to be in loving relationships.

Chapter 7 deals with healing as a transformative process for establishing a new ground of relationships. There has been a blatant disregard for our humanity. The American context has insisted that African Americans are not human beings, and therefore not entitled to healing. We have a long history of experiencing the lack of compassion, abuse of power, destruction of hope, and devastation of our lives from without and within the community. This final chapter seeks to heal our broken hearts. I encourage us to develop healthy relationships through the reestablishment of our selves as whole communal beings. My goal is healing and my hope is the development of caring relationships and the ability to draw more effectively upon African American traditions in order to inspire greater relationality and communality.

CONSIDERATIONS FOR CARING

At the close of each section, I encourage you to reflect on your relationships. At the conclusion of every chapter, points for your consideration and sample questions are provided. Take time to examine yourself, exploring the very depths of your being. As you read this book, I urge you to reflect and have conversations with others about your relationships.

- How have you understood spirituality and sexuality?

- List the things you value most in all your relation-ships. How have your understandings of spirituality and sexuality influenced your relationships?

- Do you believe it is possible to improve your relationships.

- How have memories—or experiences—of "separate and unequal" affected your life? Your relationships?

- Is spirituality higher than sexuality in your life?

- Just how important is African American spirituality for re-creating our relationships? What impact does sexuality have upon your relationships?

- "*Liberation* is the transformation to freedom, power, and authority." What does it mean to have freedom, power, and authority?

- "*Healing* is necessary for establishing a new foundation for relating." Have the hope of healing in your life.

- "*Communality* means that all people and things are inter-related." Have you understood yourself to be connected to everyone and everything? How does this understanding empower your relationships?

Chapter 2

Learning How to Relate

Beloved, let us love one another, because love is from God; everyone who loves is born of God and knows God.
— I JOHN 4:7

How does a child who has used temper tantrums later learn to negotiate compromises? Almost all children, for a long time in their lives, act out with great rage when they do not get what they want. Yet along the road to maturity, they learn to control their rage and change their behavior.

My family tells a story about one uncle's last temper tantrum. He developed the habit of holding his breath in rage. On this occasion, he held his breath and fainted. His face was then placed beneath a faucet of cold running water. That experience ended his tantrum phase. He learned to better control his rage impulses and negotiate for the things he desired.

Few transitions from tantrums are as memorable. The early years of life are the years when we learn how to relate. Everyone learns important lessons that encourage or discourage relationships. At some point, we each learn the lesson that negotiating opens doors where temper tantrums fail. The need to be in relationship with others is recognized early, even if it is only a recognition that others sometimes have what we want. We learn how to relate to individuals within the family, the entire family, the extended family, the community, and the larger social context.

Playing games is an important learning device for living. Many of the games we play as children have significance for

9

our adult lives. In fact, most children's games teach us how to live as adults. As children, we play jump rope; then as adults, we jump in and out of a variety of relationships. We play doctor, house, and commando or gangster games. As adults, we play the same games with the same rules thinking we can do what we want to whomever we want.

Remember the game hide and go seek? The game is begun by selecting a home base. I find it fascinating that many children's games have a home base. We learn very early that there is a place of security. Touching home base means that one is safe from whomever is "It." It is always to be avoided at all cost, no matter what the game. Once home base is established, the person who is It covers his or her eyes and counts while everyone else hides. Do you recall how there was always someone who did not trust It. That child lagged a little behind to make sure that It did not peek. It must never know where everyone is running to hide. Consequently, there is a level of trust that every person hiding must have. Making use of the terrain, everyone finds the best place possible to hide. After It finishes counting, he or she shouts out, "Ready or not, here I come!" Getting back to home base without being found is extremely important for those who hide. Interestingly enough, this is a game often played at dusk or at night.

This childhood game is one we continue to play as relational adults. We sometimes hide in pairs, but most often we hide alone. Even now, most of us believe that this is a game best played at night. Adulthood hide and go seek is our way of isolating ourselves from a life of openness. We sit within our hiding places hoping to find a way to get home safely. We remain in hiding, afraid to move because It might be waiting just outside the hiding place. Fearful of being exposed or hurt, we wait in our loneliness, pain, sorrow, and shame. Too many of us prefer to suffer in isolation and hope for home. Rather than taking the risk to venture out of hiding, we prefer to pretend that we do not need one another. Such fear means something is always controlling our lives, and It prevents us from being open and caring in relationships.

RACISM'S IMPACT ON OUR RELATIONSHIPS

Racism is one "It" that encourages us to remain in hiding. It seeks to exercise control over another based on racial or ethnic differences. Those differences define one group as superior and another as inferior. The racist who feels threatened by the one identified as inferior will always seek to destroy the threat through aggression and violence. When racism is It, human compassion is brought low. It encourages segregation and isolation. Those who would find unity are defensive and suspicious rather than vulnerable and trusting. As a result, racism has made it extremely difficult for African American women and men to be open and caring with one another. I will expound upon the influences of racism on our relationships in chapters 3 and 6.

We need openness and care because these are vital elements for healthy, supportive relationships. Vulnerability is a key aspect of openness, and trust is an important part of care. We can picture openness and care, but living open and caring lives is not easy. Allowing ourselves to be vulnerable and trusting requires more courage than many of us are able to admit. To be open and caring in relationships with another means freely giving oneself to another. The vulnerability and trust that are essential for open and caring relationships help to make our relationships honest, compassionate, passionate, and supportive. Because vulnerability means that a person can be severely hurt, many people are guarded and mistrustful.

Holding back thoughts and feelings are ways we hide from one another. Holding back is an act of defending ourselves from the personal devastation that can come by allowing ourselves to be open and trusting. For relationships to be caring, it is important that we learn how to relate openly.

Relating openly is not a simple task for African Americans. Not much in our collective relational American history encourages us to be open or trusting. American society has taught us that openness exposes us to danger and harm. Such vulnerability could crush our hopes and break our hearts. When we would trust someone to do better for goodness' sake, all too often we have been left in puddles from tears and pain. We long to have a faith in someone who will be self-sacrificing instead of self-serving, yet our memory tends to emphasize that others do not have our best interest at heart.

Due to our tendency not to be vulnerable and trusting, men and women generally find it extremely difficult to have supportive relationships of any type. We are often defensive out of a fear of being hurt by another. I can think of several issues that my wife and I had to work through fairly early in our marriage. Our relational histories caused us to look suspiciously at one another from time to time. I feared abandonment and she feared rejection and dishonesty. I had lots of friendships, with men and women, that I worked to maintain. She had few. We also learned different styles of relating from our families. Those different styles influenced our expectations of how we thought we should respond to one another. Although this is the first marriage for each of us, we were both previously engaged. Consequently, there are relational histories with significant others that had influenced our relationship. Every interaction taught us something about what it means to be in relationship, and every past experience influenced our relationship as a married couple.

These experiences I have identified are significant for my understanding of the condition of African American relationships. African Americans are in the throes of a relational crisis resulting from relational traumas that have been ignored. To say that we are in crisis, by definition, means that our vulnerability is heightened and our possibilities for something new are increased. Given what I have already said about our lack of desire to be vulnerable, we avoid addressing our crisis in progressive ways. The vulnerability aspect of crisis encourages us to hide from one another. This stems from a fear that others will do us harm. In fact, our crisis avoidance has us searching for new ways of defending ourselves against everyone.

Many of our relationships are based upon dishonesty and inappropriate expectations of what others will do. Like children who discover that temper tantrums are not the best way to get what they want, we learn how to present ourselves to get what we selfishly want for ourselves. We mask our feelings and desires to satisfy our selfish desires. Our inappropriate expectations come from believing that every man or woman wants only one thing. One result of such beliefs is that we seek to prove that men or women indeed want only one thing. Once we have forced the other to conform to our understandings, we say, "I knew it all along. You are just like every other woman [or man]." Our personal fears of vulnerability become another person's defeat as we negotiate our relationships.

A crisis creates possibilities by helping people to come together, positively and negatively, under the pressure of crippling change. Here are two examples. First, when a tragedy occurs within a community, that tragedy has a way of gathering the community in collective cooperation. If the tragedy had not occurred, the community might not otherwise gather in any collective, supportive way. Second, a loss can gather and unite a family in ways that it might not otherwise gather during the course of a year. Funerals are often impromptu family reunions for much of the African American community. Also, the death of a loved one can encourage feuding family members to negotiate their differences.

An illustration of crisis negatively bringing people together is gang life. The gangster life means to constantly live in crisis resulting from trauma. Given the way I am defining crisis, one could conclude that gang activity is so strong because gang casualties are so high. Understanding that gangs are structured as families with their own set of family values means the high mortality rate of members strengthens the bond rather than decreases the gang activity. The survival of the family (gang) at any cost is what becomes important. The tragedy of loss unites the group through funeral rituals. The survival needs send them out to engage in destructive behavior as a way of coping with the vulnerability.

Sometimes the nature of our relationships seems to be that we consider men as a gang and women as a rival gang. We regularly strive against one another to preserve our particular gang. We develop rituals to compensate for our sense of loss of power and authority. And we attack one another as a way of covering our vulnerability. Recognizing this type of reaction to crisis can actually help us to develop healthier ways of relating to one another as men and women.

USING PASTORAL PSYCHOLOGY TO INTERPRET OUR RELATIONSHIPS

African American pastoral psychology is an important discipline for interpreting our relationships. As a general approach, pastoral psychology is a free-standing discipline like clinical psychology or developmental psychology. Yet pastoral psychology is a theological discipline. It begins with the understanding that humanity has been created in the image and likeness of God, and God cares for our well-being. Its concern for the divine-human relationship means it tends to stand alone among other helping approaches. It helps us to reflect in ways that other approaches do not consider.

The discipline's attentiveness to the divine-human relationship prompts a concern for faith issues. Therefore, it is attentive to the questions of what it means to live as a faith community. Because pastoral psychology is a theological discipline, it employs biblical texts and Christian understandings as primary sources for reflection. Naturally, psychological theories are also employed, but they are basically used as interpretive tools for exploring the human condition and analyzing the pains of life.[1]

The most prominent American approaches to pastoral psychology seek to eliminate human suffering one person at a time. They are attentive to the oppressions experienced in life, but are not always interested in bringing liberation. As we consider African American relationships, a pastoral psychology that does not give attention to liberation will not transform relational crises. The traumas associated with African American suffering must be addressed with liberation as the goal. Our suffering does not involve just the pains of loss and transitions that are a part of growth. Our suffering also includes the traumas caused by individuals, institutional racism, and sexism. We suffer due to class struggles resulting from chronic economic problems. We struggle to keep our hopes alive for something better. Yet we live with the constant fear that the better will never be attained.[2]

Here is a situation I think helpful for illustrating the value of African American pastoral psychology. I was one of three men standing on the northbound platform awaiting a commuter train. It was an above-ground, open-air station with no clocks. A young African American woman exited a train on the southbound platform. Walking to exit the station, she hailed one of the European American men on the northbound side and asked him for the time. "Excuse me," she called. "Excuse me, sir. Do you have the time?" He looked at her but said nothing. With no vocal response from the man, she asked again in a frustrated voice, "Excuse me. Do *you* have the time?" After his refusal to acknowledge her request, she proceeded to curse him.

The second European American man on the northbound platform was asked the same question in a very polite way. Rather than answering her question, he proceeded to ridicule her for her behavior. He completely ignored the silence of the first man who provoked her anger. To the second man she declared, "He looked at me and chose to ignore me." And she asked again, "Do *you* have the time?" After his refusal to acknowledge her question, she declared him rude and in need of an attitude adjustment. When she walked past my position, she neither asked for the time nor did she present me with the same attitude that she had just displayed to the previous two men. Instead, she greeted me in a family-like fashion and inquired about my day.

How should we understand this woman's reaction? What had she learned about relating to others? One could conclude that she is rude, angry, and ignorant. I believe if we declare her rude, we misinterpret the whole situation. Was it that she could not get what she wanted so she had an adult tantrum? We should not focus on her because of her outburst. We should consider how she was provoked by the rudeness of the first two men. Whatever one considers regarding this situation, it should not exclude considering the influences of racism and sexism.

From an African American pastoral psychological approach, this woman was raging against nonexistence. Her being ignored by the first two men was not just a matter of declaring her unworthy of an answer; it was a declaration that she did not exist as a human being. Had the first man answered her polite question, she would have moved on. He ignored her. They were on separate platforms divided by two sets of train tracks. Did he think her question was her panhandler lead-in even as she was a platform away?

The second man who was asked could have answered her, but he felt himself morally superior and also ignored her question. Instead of giving an answer, he lectured her on her behavior. He completely ignored the rudeness of the first man and focused only on the woman's behavior. He judged this black woman and absolved the white man. She once again defended herself. The fact that she did not ask me for the time was evidence that being told the time was not the most important part of our exchange. What was most important was the human interaction and the acknowledgment of her existence. She addressed me respectfully and with familiarity to declare she was not rude or ignorant. Her rage was due to the innumerable experiences that would deny her being. Her rage became her vitality, it became her teaching moment to declare that she is *ALIVE*. Yet, she will be looked at in the future and asked, "Why are you so angry?" And the behavior of the men will not be given a second thought.

BLACK THEOLOGY AND "PROTRACTED TRAUMATIC STRESS DISORDER"

The African in America has a strong heritage, but our experience has been mingled with evil and suffering. What we have learned about relationships requires that a specifically African American understanding of life be developed. This approach needs to be sensitive to the lessons we have learned about life and relationships. It needs to consider the information that has been passed on from generation to generation.

We are in need of healing. Our lives have been turned upside down and inside out. Our pain seems to have more power in determining our course than the communal characteristics that once dominated our understanding of relationship. When pain is the primary motivator in relationship, human conduct is guided by inflicting pain, reacting to pain, and avoiding openness. We need to learn to make choices based upon a desire for healthy relationships. Our African heritage is directed toward communal relationships, but the pain of our past directs us to hide. If we are going to conquer the pain and end the suffering, every approach to the African in America must be communal based, survival directed, and healing oriented. African American pastoral psychology can help us get back to home base.

Although pastoral psychology is a part of the theological enterprise, not all theological perspectives or theories of human transformation are African American appropriate. If pastoral psychology fails to focus on African American liberation when considering the African American community, then it will perpetuate the so-called incog*negro* syndrome. That is, we have not a clue of who we are nor where we come from.

Such a failure will also maintain the painful condition of "protracted traumatic stress disorder." This condition is a modification of the clinical diagnosis called post-traumatic stress disorder. Post-traumatic stress disorder tends to be configured around a single life-threatening event that communicates that life is unsafe and uncertain. It presumes that there is an event in the past that produces an array of behavioral symptoms to be treated.[3]

When others have diagnosed African Americans as having post-traumatic stress, the result has been a focus on American "slavocracy." Some have used that interpretation to say that slavery is in the past and we need to get over it. However, contrary to popular opinion, our trauma is not a single event, like slavery, that could be considered in the past. We are traumatized daily, which means our suffering is protracted. The pain of our protracted existence must be arrested and our condition transformed by healing.

While an essential component of African American pastoral psychology is African spirituality, black theology is a critical resource for healing the wounded African American soul. Black theology forces us to explore our experience with evil while maintaining a focus on the presence of God within the African American. Our protracted traumatic existence means that evil and suffering continue to inform and impact our lives. Without the resources of African American spirituality and black theology, our hopes for change are limited. Our spirituality compels us, and black theology declares that we shall be free, someday. Our inspired imagination gives us hope for today and tomorrow.

We are living a "protracted traumatic" existence characterized by acts of racism, sexism, classism, violence, and institutional sabotage. The woman at the train was not experiencing racism and sexism as a post-traumatic experience. She continues to experience racism in an ongoing protracted traumatic way. The remaining chapters look specifically at several aspects of our protracted traumatic existence. Our historical self is being distorted by false images of who we are. They encourage communal disconnection and ultimately result in broken relationships. This condition has us searching to find ways to say we exist and have value. It has us searching for home, safety, and security.

CONSIDERATIONS FOR CARING

- Have you learned how to control your rage in relationship?

- Think about ways you hide in your relationships. How fearful are you to trust another?

Reflect on the following situations as indicators of your level of vulnerability and trust:

- Think of your most personal, best kept secret. Is there anyone with whom you can share that secret?

If your answer is no, why don't you trust anyone enough to share your most personal thoughts? If your answer is yes, how do you know you can trust that person with your most personal thoughts?

- Think about the emotion you are least likely to express in public. What attitudes are associated with openly expressing that emotion? What is your worst fear associated with the public expression of that emotion?

- How important is it to you that the broader structures of injustice and liberation be addressed in your life and community?

- Think about your past experiences. How have your family life and past relationships influenced your present relationships with family, friends, and significant other?

- Does "protracted traumatic stress disorder" help to make sense of your experiences? Of your family's experiences?

- In what ways are you searching for home, safety, and security?

Chapter 3

Searching for a Place to Call Home

So Sarah said to Abraham, "Cast out this slave woman with her son; for the son of this slave woman shall not inherit along with my son Isaac." —GENESIS 21:10

For I know that nothing good dwells within me, that is, in my flesh.... Wretched [hu]man that I am! Who will rescue me from this body of death? —ROMANS 7:18A, 24

So we are always confident; even though we know that while we are at home in the body we are away from the Lord.... Yes, we do have confidence, and we would rather be away from the body and at home with the Lord.
—2 CORINTHIANS 5:6, 8

The activities of each generation affect the lives of the generations that follow. Everyone has been influenced by the lives of those who have walked ahead of us. Our present attitudes have been shaped by those who first lived the African American experience. Parents influence children, and older siblings influence younger siblings. Acts of protest and violence affect those directly involved as well as those who were not present. What we do today will influence the lives of those who will be responsible tomorrow.

I was born in 1959, which means my thoughts have been influenced and shaped by the variety of reformative activities of the 1960s. During that time, we were returning to natural hair styles that were later modified with "blow-out kits." We wore dashikis and berets as fashion statements that represented a new social consciousness. With clenched fists raised high, we stood in protest against the forces of oppression. We stated loudly, "I'm black, and I'm proud." We identified racism as the evil system to be eliminated. Attitudes were confronted, and laws were changed. These activities were also accompanied by death. Leaders were assassinated, and shoot-outs occurred between opposing groups. Government investigators and local police were among the opposition. Churches were bombed and innocent people died. We were engaged in a race conflict inside our borders and an "armed conflict" in Southeast Asia. We watched *Ozzie and Harriet* and saw how the other side lived.

The sixties were also the time of desegregation and integration, but this occurred before there was an actual liberation. I was bussed from my black neighborhood out to the white suburbs. Two experiences from those days stick out in my mind. The first happened during recess. Someone pinched one of my classmates. When he turned, he saw me with my back turned to him and assumed I pinched him. He began to throw punches at me, and I didn't understand why. Naturally, I defended myself. When the teacher saw the two of us squared off, she grabbed me and accused me of instigating the whole thing because I was the "inner city" black child. The second occurred in the classroom with the same teacher. She answered a question about current affairs by identifying Martin Luther King Jr. as a "troublemaker." She said nothing about the obvious injustices. She said nothing about what nonviolent protesters were protesting. Her answer was nothing more than a comment about her sense of social discomfort. Many situations like those highlighted during my childhood illustrate the significance of skin color in American society. Numerous experiences like those mentioned lead me to explore race relations and the impact of racism upon our relationships.

The black consciousness movement of the 1960s sought to transform the ideas and images of what it meant to be black and African in America. The norm of the society has been that white is pure and good. The lighter or the whiter something is, the better that something is—whether flour, sugar, or precious metals. This resulted in an incredible amount of shame and disgust associated with being a dark-skinned person. All of the negative ideas and associations with the color black were associated with people of African descent. During the slavery period in the United States, African equaled slave and sexual immorality. In the twentieth century, black meant poverty, sexual prowess, and criminal behavior. Anyone who was identified as "a credit to the race" was someone whose behaviors exemplified whiteness. Even intelligence has been understood as a white virtue.

In the sixties, it was not unusual for someone to say, "If you're white, you're all right. If you're yellow, you're mellow. If you're brown, stick around. If you're black, get back." White represented pride, privilege, and power. It was the mission of black consciousness to turn the negatives into positives. All the disgust was turned upside down. Black pride led the way for people to believe that "black is beautiful." Rather than hiding from the sun for fear of being called "midnight," we basked in the sun saying, "The blacker the berry, the sweeter the juice." On the surface, black was in. Beneath the surface, however, black as shameful continued to assert an influence.

Try as we might, we still carried many feelings that white was better. Being a darker child, I was still called "Oreo," not because I was thought to be black acting white, but because I was so dark. My schoolmates frequently identified me as being "too" dark. Ironically, this was done to me by those who supposedly took great pride in being black. The opposite end of the color spectrum within the black community also suffered the consequences of these differing attitudes. Lighter-skinned blacks were often not recognized as one of those "down for the cause" because their skin was not dark enough. What is more distressing is that these same attitudes are still alive and well today. My wife was told that she should not marry me because I was so dark. Those giving this advice sought to justify their position by adding that she really needed to think about what our children would look like. My wife, of course, thought it was absolutely crazy because her father and I were formed from the same dark clay.

These are the feelings and attitudes that we continue to deal with as blacks in America. All African Americans have struggled with color issues from one perspective or another. There is no single story that has the capacity to illustrate our color-conscious reality to us. It is our lived experience to which each of us can respond, "Say no more. I know!" The United States is not color-blind and we are not color-insensitive. We live with the constant awareness of our black bodies. Unfortunately, our awareness is not always a comfortable home.

THE BLACK BODY

As African Americans, we face a difficult task to be "at home in our own skin." We have social and relational pressures that constantly challenge our ideas of comfort and acceptability. We have never been fully accepted in the United States, and accepting ourselves has been problematic at best. We have an overwhelmingly negative history of what it has meant to be black in America. The African identity has been constantly degraded as savage and backward. We have also been associated with cannibalism, Tarzan, and King Kong. We have been continually bombarded with degrading ideas, for example, that we should be grateful that we were delivered from living in the trees. Furthermore, Africa has been identified as progressive only where the advancements have been attributed to Europeans in Africa. Consequently, if we are not conscientious, our dark bodies can feel like jailhouses of shame and ostracism rather than homes of warmth and compassion.

Like it or not, we have made the body the center of many of our problems. Too often, we experience life as prisoners of our American color consciousness, incarcerated in earthen mud bodies. Because we cannot just "jump out of our skin," we live frustrated lives with relationship problems. We want our bodies to be home base, but the shame associated with black skin has us hiding from the demoralizing "It." Somehow, we have come to believe that if we can just get our black body issues under control, all of our relationship problems related to maleness/femaleness, masculinity/femininity, and manhood/womanhood would be resolved. This is a part of our human condition as African Americans. We have a complicated history with our black skin that covers our "problematic bodies." The truth we need to come to terms with is this: if we cannot be at home in our own skin, we cannot be at home with another.

At the turn of the twentieth century, W. E. B. Du Bois had much to say about the African American condition. His classic statement from *The Souls of Black Folks* declares: "It is a peculiar sensation, this double-consciousness, this sense of always looking at one's self through the eyes of others ... one ever feeling his [her] two-ness—an American, a Negro; two souls, two thoughts, two unreconciled strivings; two warring ideals in one dark body." This double-consciousness, as he understood it, was created by the knife of racism. Du Bois saw African Americans as fractured, disjointed, and confused regarding who we are and, perhaps, clueless regarding who we ought to be. We interpret the double-consciousness to be related to color issues exclusively; however color is not the only place where this sense of two-ness expresses itself. The two-ness is also experienced in our bodily issues as relationship problems.

While we must deal with racism's pronouncements upon our black skin and all of its implications for our social and economic security, we also find ourselves in a peculiar and precarious condition with regard to our male and female relationships. Racism's pronouncements about our character have been enmeshed with our struggle to identify what it means to be gendered adults in relationship with one another. Many of our ideas of manhood, womanhood, and relational roles have been shaped by our reactions to racist images and ideas. Our discomfort with our black bodies is evidence of Du Bois's "two warring ideals" in not one but "two dark bodies," one male and one female. Both ideas are negative. We have one set of ideas about the black man and a different set of ideas about the black woman, yet both sets of ideas put men and women at odds with one another.

Racism has taught us to be uncomfortable with ourselves. The color black is not associated with home in any positive way. The creation of a home, therefore, is an exhausting task. Our relationships are governed by power differentials and power plays. U.S. slavery set up a racial caste system, which continues to influence our relationships. Our interactions tend to be controlled externally by negative images and forces dictated by a dominant hierarchical culture. While a high degree of mutuality has fostered our survival in the U.S., we have been inclined to live according to superior/inferior roles. We have imitated the dominant culture's norms for relationship rather than clinging to the ideas that brought us through our hardships. This is so ironic. The black body is almost always seen as inferior, the exceptions being athletic and sexual performance, yet we reproduce an unequal system for ourselves.

The African American experience has been a struggle to find a place to call home. The lack of positive regard for blackness and black bodies has led to African American mental and emotional homelessness. The unrelenting negative regard for African and African American men and women has perpetuated spiritual homelessness among African Americans. Spirituality makes whole and holy human beings, but we are fractured searching for wholeness and a home.

There are a variety of adages and clichés associated with home. We say, "Home, sweet home,"and, "Be it ever so humble, there's no place like home." When we welcome a guest who is a friend, we say, "Make yourself at home." Our wanderings have caused us to say that "home is where the heart is," which is nuanced by "home is wherever you are." Dionne Warwick and Luther Vandross told several generations, "A chair is not a house, and a house is not a home when the two of us are apart and one of us has a broken heart." So, as we can see, home carries meanings of peace and relationship that we express in our physical being. But it does not stop with our physicality. We also have spiritual associations with the concept of home: we are pilgrims in this world and Heaven is our home. Consequently, home is the place "where the wicked shall cease from troubling and the Sabbath shall have no end." Others say, "I've got a home in Gloryland that outshines the sun." When these statements are placed in the midst and context of African American life, we often describe ourselves as wanderers in the wilderness, far from the places of peace, and cut off from loving-kindness. We are searching for a place called home.

THE SEARCH FOR HOME

Home is a significant metaphor of life. It not only represents our residential dwelling place of warmth and security, comfort and stability; home represents—psychologically and spiritually—the body. Because home is ever longed for, many of us nomadically and energetically search for it. Largely, that is why many people bounce from relationship to relationship: they are engaged in a sacred search for home in another. They want to find that one person who brings a sigh of relief. We all want to say, "Ah, I'm home." Those of us who were entertained by "I Love Lucy" don't enjoy saying, "Lucy, I'm home!" just to laugh at Ricky Ricardo. We repeat the statement because it is what we desire. We long to be home.

For many African Americans, searching for home in another means finding someone with "good" hair of the right length, with the right skin color, who talks the right way, with the right attitude, who holds the right kind of job and owns the right possessions. Our quest for the "good life" is our attempt to be safe at home. We understand the fulfillment of love to be permanently located in a comforting space we call home.

We engage in this search for home as though it is a scene to be set on a stage. We have a false idea that if we can simply position the proper stage props, we can have an instant home. With this understanding, the lack of home means someone's body is not properly positioned on the stage. It also means someone has been made into an object for the purpose of creating one's mood or fantasy. The objectified person loses her or his individuality and uniqueness for the purpose of fulfilling a role for another's comfort. This staging can be heard when people complain, "If 'they' would just act like a real _____," or "If 'they' would just act 'right,' then we would not have these problems." Acting like what one is not becomes a key factor in relationship when someone is made an object for the purpose of creating home.

Recognizing that life and love are what every person longs for and needs, we often assume the process of finding home to be simple. Unfortunately, it is never simple or easy, particularly for African Americans. This is due to the fact that we have not recognized the complexity of our relationships. What is often overlooked is that Africans in America have a legacy to contend with that has been insistent that we not find a home—in America, within ourselves, or with one another. Very little within our historical social experience has encouraged us to be relationally committed. We have a long history we carry within our soul of forcibly being ripped from those we love, denied humanity and community, denied the opportunity for marriage and spousal protection, and prohibited from providing familial security.

Here is our living legacy as African Americans: we have lived socially vulnerable lives. We have lived without much protection. The earliest laws were written to prevent us from having the rights to life, liberty, and property. We have been tormented, tortured, maimed, murdered, raped, degraded, and humiliated without legal recourse against the inhumane treatment we have received. Our survival has been a modern miracle. Through it all, we have been able to maintain the strength of African communality. Unfortunately, this has not been sufficient to overcome our interpersonal relational difficulties.

Many of our relationships have been maintained by sacrificing significant parts of our humanity. Rather than nurturing our men and women in community, we have sacrificed one another and called it the process of creating community. An example from our past that expresses this sacrificial behavior comes from the civil rights/black power movement. Racism was declared to be the social evil to be fought against collectively. When women desired that the issue of sexism be a part of the platform, men insisted that racism was a larger, more significant issue. This resulted in women sacrificing their concerns for liberation within the African American community and womanhood being sacrificed for "the cause."

Many of us have been operating under the assumption that male/female relationships, regardless of cultural background, are male/female relationships. There has been an unspoken belief that relationships have a universal quality. In chapters 4–6, I talk specifically about how the dominant culture has a set of rules regarding relationships between men and women that have worked against us. The ideas that have been good for some within the dominant culture have not always been good for African Americans. Our history in community, family, and manhood/womanhood has differed. Even when there has been a recognition that there is something culturally different about African American men and women in relationship, the dominant culture has failed to account accurately for the hidden messages we live with.

The dominant culture has tended to conclude that we have the inability to maintain commitments due to the weaknesses of our family structure. I will examine this point at some length in chapter 5. In addition to the negative attitudes about our families, there is a whole host of messages that deny our human goodness and force us apart. How many cultures the world over are as verbally abusive of men and women as African Americans can sometimes be? In comedy, music, and movies, we display a blatant disrespect for our relationships in the name of "keeping it real." What is it about our reality that causes us to degrade one another the way we do?

There is a twisted story beneath our statement of longing for home that is destructive of our relationships. Our longing sends us searching, but the corruption that exists beneath the surface sabotages our interactions. We make statements that describe the good qualities we want; then we seek to dominate or destroy what we have declared as our desire. This is seen in the man who desires to sleep with as many women as he can, but wants to marry a "good" woman who has slept with no other. It is seen in the woman who wants a "strong" man, but wants to dominate his every action due to a lack of trust. Consequently, if we are going to overcome the power of the hidden messages, we must understand their deep imprint upon our lives and why we search for the things we do in another.

Where do these messages come from, and why do they continue to have power in our lives? In this regard, it is imperative that we look to the past to understand our present condition. Relationally, we all know that our past experiences, particularly our negative past experiences, affect our relational choices. There are reasons why everyone is attracted to the same types of friends and lovers. Our tendency, however, is to consider such attractions only in the context of our individual lifetimes. We conclude that we are seeking to be in relationship with people who resemble our fathers and mothers or the same types of people who have always been our friends. Yet, if we limit our view to our personal, individual experiences, we overlook our inherited behaviors and experiences as a people.

Believing our inherited behaviors and experiences have power in our lives is not a far-fetched notion. We recognize that many of our behaviors as African Americans extend beyond our current contexts. We know that the different things we do result from family history. This history can sometimes be traced to roots in the South, but always extends back to Africa. Therefore, it is important that we reflect historically and biblically on our relationships. African Americans have a long history of suffering; and we are religious people who have been influenced by the Bible. With this in mind, I believe it is important that we consider our lives before we became Americans. Because negative experiences do have real power in our lives, we need to rethink our difficulties. Many of them began with our experiences in the dungeons of Cape Coast, Ghana, and the Middle Passage. The biblical narrative I find significant for helping us to rethink our relationships is the Ishmael narrative of Genesis, which will be discussed later in this chapter.

The dungeons and Middle Passage experiences are influential components in the identity formation of African Americans. They are critical historical touch points that continue to have an impact on how we come to understand our relationships as men and women. The dungeons and Middle Passage are the headwaters of our social and relational vulnerability. The physical structures of the dungeons, along with the physical, mental, and emotional traumas of the dungeons and deportation, have made it extremely difficult for us to find home with one another.

The Hagar/Ishmael/Abraham/Sarah story is a biblical narrative that is close to our experience in the U.S. The narrative expresses abuse, abandonment, bondage, faith, lament, and survival. It expresses what it means to be an outcast searching for a place to call home. Cape Coast and the Middle Passage experiences combined with the biblical narrative reveal the depth of our difficulty as well as the possibility for renegotiating our deliverance and liberation.

The reality of the pain and shame of the dungeons and Middle Passage is probably obvious. Most of us know about the brutality resulting from our deportation from Africa. The problem is, perhaps, seeing the connections between our experience and the Ishmael narrative. When we consider the narrative, most of us cling to Abraham, Sarah, and Isaac, whereas the possibility of our deliverance rests in our experiential identification with Hagar and Ishmael. The fact is that most African Americans have known the pain of Hagar, who was taken from her home and experienced the full range of abuses of power. We have also known the pain of Ishmael, who was kicked out of his home when he had outlived his usefulness. We have known the pain associated with feeling there is no one present as our protector and provider in the times of need or trouble. We have very little that reinforces the notion that we can depend on one another to be our home.

JAIL VERSUS HOME

While on a study tour in Ghana, West Africa, during the summer of 1997, I walked through the dungeons of Elmina and Cape Coast castles, two fortresses with ports from which were launched many ships filled with Africans as human cargo. Elmina, the oldest dungeon fortress, was completed in 1561. My tours of those two places continue to have the power to evoke strong emotional reactions within me. I witnessed the spaces and places of absolute horror that were endured by my African ancestors. As I walked from courtyard to corridor and from room to room, I observed and processed every bit of information. And because I was not emotionally detached, I experienced every horrifying story. It was as though the spirits of those who suffered were there confirming every atrocity and communicating their feelings of terror and isolation. The experience made a connection within my soul that assaulted my humanity. The design of the building—identified by some as a castle and others as a dungeon—was diabolical. The purpose of the dungeon experience was to degrade and distort the souls of Africans. The guiding ideology was European religion, the systematic oppression was psychological, and the result was more than a loss of dignity: it was a loss of self.

We walked through both Elmina and Cape Coast dungeons on the same day. Our Elmina tour began with a history of its construction and the identification of the nations that fought to control the space. We were told how African men and women were physically separated from one another. After the general information, we then proceeded to the women's dungeon, where we were told of the numbers that were cramped into two small rooms for days or months. They ate and relieved themselves in pots. They slept on the floor. All these activities were done in the same space, in which no comfort was known. They were paraded in the courtyards outside their cells, where the officers would pick the women they wanted to rape. The women's cells were on the first level and the officers' quarters were on the second level. A special stairway was constructed so the officers would have direct access to the women. Imagine hearing the screams of familiar voices—friends, sisters, mothers, cousins—not far from where you are standing and being unable to save them from being raped. Imagine the torture and abuse and being powerless to intervene. The people were incarcerated and then dehumanized.

The officers' quarters were above the dungeons, but more significantly the church within the fortress was built directly in the center above the men's dungeons. Worship and confession were at the center of the pain and dehumanization. It is no wonder that many have described Christianity as the "white man's religion." This industry of misery was carried out by "the faithful" with the blessings of church officials. The screams of torment and the smell of death were without end. Isolation and total submission to the will of another became the all-pervasive ethos—submit or die. The history the tour guides shared made it very clear that the captives were unable to protect, defend, rescue, or comfort one another.

The final steps of our walk through this outrage were to the "door of no return." We were directed from the cells through the passageways that our ancestors walked to be boarded onto ships. No doubt, the captives thought they were headed for hell. The boarding was typically done at night. While one might conclude that boarding was carried out simply according to the changing of the tides, it served the deconstructing efforts of the slavers. To move the Africans through these corridors under the cover of darkness served to disorient them and deepen the traumatic experience. The boarding became another veil hung between who we were and what the slavers desired us to be. This was the long walk that preceded chattel enslavement. To be identified as chattel meant we had no rights as human beings. We were identified as less than human. With heads shaved and skin branded by hot irons, we were stripped naked and led through this narrow door; there was no returning to a life that was once known in the places we called home.

On board ship, African men and women were again placed in separate holds—the men chained below deck in leg irons and the women and children on the upper deck. While both were demoralized, dehumanized, and brutalized, the women were sexually exploited. Their nakedness was a constant reminder of their sexual vulnerability. Many African women landed on these shores already impregnated by a dungeon captor or crew member. The general nature of relationships holds that bodies are to be covenantally committed to one another. We are to be protective of the family unit. The Middle Passage experience, however, made relational unity an impossibility. We were regarded as bodies without feeling, families, or history. One of our earliest social impulses as human beings is to say no. Yet, we were denied that inalienable right. Our no was not respected. Many times when we wanted to say no, we were forced to say yes.

It is not easy for men or women to accept, to give, or to receive after the experiences of such brutalization. While women seem to be more inclined to have the emotional capacity to share "in spite of," men tend to be accepting and nurturing only of what they perceive as pure. We men are sometimes able to move beyond this tendency, though often with emotional difficulty. With such powerful notions of purity, to be able to love even our own children men frequently need to see women as pure. This notion has had a profound impact upon the attitudes that African American men project upon African American women. Men negatively see women as a "piece" to satisfy their desires for pleasure. Sometimes it even seems that the attitude is, "If she were pure, she would not get pregnant when we go to bed together." Without purity, there is no commitment. While men often have issues with purity, women often have issues with power. Many women see men as powerless outside of sexual relations, and ironically see sex as men's weakness. Women negatively think that if they can control a man's sexuality, they can control his life. These attitudes have placed emotional distance between men and women.

Again, this was diabolical and systematic evil. The Middle Passage was a time of brainwashing and indoctrination. It was the slavers' "job" to transform free, spirit-filled Africans into passionless "docile slaves." Their purpose was to destroy human dignity through removal of names and status; to destroy relationships through reinforcing vulnerability and creating undesirability; and to destroy identity through the erasure of African culture and history. Nakedness, rape, chains, and beatings were the first stages of the destruction of our relationships.

I must admit, having seen the movie *Sankofa,* when we began our tour at Cape Coast dungeon I was a little concerned that I would be transported through time as the movie's main character was. At both Elmina and Cape Coast, I walked to every corner of every space, except in the churches. The holiest ground was the space that had been occupied by our African ancestors. Although I went into no trance, if I see pictures of those places today, I am immediately overwhelmed by the feelings I experienced there.

The dungeons on the coast of Ghana and the Middle Passage were engineered to systematically separate Africans from their relational understanding of manhood, womanhood, family, community, and humanity. The means to that end were physical, social, psychological, and political. I believe we are still living with the vestiges of those experiences and structures. Consider our present social and relational situation as interpreted through the experiences of the past. Before our enslavement, we had a highly sophisticated understanding of community, family, and social responsibility. All of these relationships were informed by our understanding of humanity. Our enslavement, however, distorted our relationships, causing us to abuse rather than support one another. Those experiences also informed how we feel about being close to one another.

TRANSFORMING SPACE AND SPACE RELATIONSHIPS

Space relationships are a very important part of human interaction. The distance we establish between one another helps us to maintain our sense of safety and security. When we feel that another person has gotten too close, we back away to a safer space relationship. People consciously invade the space of another when they choose to be aggressive. We get as close as we can without touching in an effort to intimidate one another because a person's personal space is sacred. We violate others' space in an effort to destroy their resistance. This is why Africans were forced to occupy cramped spaces. One body constantly pressing another, with no private space, resulted in the loss of self. This is also why the women were sexually violated. Both violations of space were intended to communicate that there is nothing sacred about the African self.

When our space is violated in this manner, we will either fight or try to escape to recover our sense of safety and selfhood. Because our space has been violated as African American men and women, we are both fighting and escaping. Our acts of violence are out of control, and our escaping behaviors are just as destructive. We all know the litany of violence in our communities as well as the many ways we try to run away from our problems. We are fighting and escaping in our attempts to recover our sense of safety and selfhood. Our efforts, however, are destroying our relationships in much the same way the dungeons and Middle Passage destroyed our relationships.

Of course, there are persons in our lives to whom we desire to be very close, and there are persons from whom we cannot find enough space to distance ourselves. Space relationships offer us comfort and assurance. They make a statement about our confidence and self-worth. If we know our personal space to be sacred, we are more easily connected to the Holy. Also, if we acknowledge personal space to be sacred, the quality of our relationships changes because we understand ourselves to be in sacred relationships.

Consider the large number of African American men in prisons. Jail has become the substitute for home. We are still living and dying under the influence of the West African dungeon experience. We have been socially programmed for jail, estrangement, and genocide. Seemingly, we believe the only life we can have is the one we have been shown through our captivity. In the past, we were jailed in dungeons, cargo holds, slavocracy. We are now right back in the dungeons, only this time it is the American penal system and the cells of isolation we construct that reveal our unwillingness to be open and trusting. We are submitting to a vicious cycle of genocidal impulses. We are dying by our own hands from a system set in motion more than five hundred years ago.

Many of us have been able to overcome the victimization of our past and avoid the jails. Our capacity to avoid has come from our believing there is a force more powerful than the system that seeks our destruction. Where a strong sense of relationship and the sacredness of the self has been reinforced, there you will find a person with a strong character who is committed to family, friendship, community, and faith. These persons have a value system that chooses life in relationship above individual survival. The prison industry can be described as a racist conspiracy, but the plot can be stopped by choosing to emphasize relationships. Racism is life-denying. It can be conquered only by choosing human life in the face of the death called racism.

The imprisonment of African American men has also had a devastating impact on African American women and their vulnerabilities. The dungeons and Middle Passage experiences were determined to make African women completely vulnerable, without protection or having a sense of sacred selfhood. The imprisonment of our young men continues to maintain that legacy of vulnerability and irreverence for African American women. We live in a patriarchal society that continues to assign the role of protection to men. If the men are imprisoned, the perception is that women are unprotected and easy prey. We continue to be physically separated and violate one another's space through our words and attitudes. Sheltering one another from the brutalities of the world is rarely a thought of our minds.

If we look at the historical foundations of our relationships, it is not difficult to see why we treat one another the ways we do. When we look at our relationships through the lenses of the dungeons and Middle Passage, it is no surprise that African American women and men are searching for home. Women have made reclaiming sacred selfhood a high priority due to the violations of their bodies. Men continue to struggle with issues of control and respect because of their inability to function as patriarchs in a patriarchal world. This also makes it easier for us to understand why we have the sex and gender identities we do. The degree to which our gender identities have been constructed around the experience of our brutalization affects all of our relationships—brother/sister, covenantal, familial, communal, and societal.

THE COLORING OF OUR RELATIONSHIPS

We have been conditioned to perceive white as pure and black, not just as dirty, but evil. When we associate colors with attitudes, black tends to have negative meanings. Issues of morality frequently get painted in black or white. If we must lie, we prefer our lies to be "little white lies." Many merchants see black shoppers as a threat, but they can hardly wait for "Black Friday," the day after Thanksgiving, to boost their annual sales. Yes, a "black tie affair" will be an evening of elegance, but we are encouraged to avoid black moods. We long for the white dress, white picket fence, and white God. Who among us does not want what is good and pure? More importantly, how do these perceptions of colors influence our relationships?

The various statements we make about the colors black and white are regularly applied to dating relationships. Without a doubt, we do not live in a color-blind society. What impact has the issue of white purity and black evil really had upon our choices of whom to date? We say that a choice of a white person by a black person has to do with our desire for the forbidden fruit, to get even with white men, or to elevate our social status. When a white person chooses a black person, we say, "Once you go black, you can never go back," or "The white person is just fulfilling a fantasy." Sometimes the explanation is as simple as these typical attitudes, but other times the coupling of black men with white women is more than just picking forbidden fruit or retaliating against white men. Sometimes the coupling of black women with white men is more than just picking forbidden fruit or compensating for the lack of available black men. Our history makes it easy for us to draw these typical conclusions, but there are those among us who have found true love and companionship in black and white.

Here I am looking specifically at African American relationships. I believe there are some issues at the center of our African American being that negatively affect our relationships. Earlier I suggested there are hidden messages within us that force us apart. What if the foundation of our relationships is that black men have an unconscious perception that black women have been soiled by rape and are evil because of their black skin? And what if that foundation includes an unconscious perception on the part of black women that black men are impotent and unable to defend them or provide security for them, financial or otherwise? If these perceptions are just beneath the surface influencing our relationships, it is no wonder that we have so much trouble communicating with one another. Some time ago, a couple in my extended family was having a little spat. During the course of the disagreement, the husband said to the wife, "You are a clever negress, aren't you?" No matter how many ways you examine his question, it was an insult. He could have said far worse, but where did the attitude for this insult originate?

Reforming the foundation of our relationships could do much to restore the selfhood that was lost in the dungeons and Middle Passage. We need to radically change our perceptions of who we are, who we believe others to be, and the ways we relate to one another. While I believe African Americans have had strong systems of resistance, we have also had patterns of destruction woven into our relational fabric. The separation and isolation impulses that energetically influence our relationships are intended to imprison us and prevent us from ever finding home. Our liberation from our legacy of incarceration will return us to selfhood and turn us toward one another.

We are acting upon impulses that are deeply seated within the reservoirs of our mental and emotional histories. Yet we can be free from the power of the past. Our liberation and salvation rest on our ability to see that our behaviors are based upon a distorted image of ourselves and our relationships. Once we are able to see that we are relying on negative images and opinions designed to destroy us, we can develop new and positive images that will nurture our relationships. We are caught in the vale of tears on this side of the Middle Passage. Many of us are paralyzed with no understanding of why we cannot get together as family, friends, and lovers. Many of us are totally confused about who we are and how to care for one another.

HAGAR AND ISHMAEL'S SEARCH FOR HOME

The story of our lives as African Americans is very close to the biblical narrative of the enslaved Egyptian woman named Hagar and her son, Ishmael. Their life circumstances made it very difficult for them to find the home they desired. Although we know more about Abraham, Sarah, Hagar, and Isaac than we do about Ishmael from this story, I believe there is much to be learned from Ishmael's story as we reflect on African American relationships. Just as a reflection on our history can tell us much about why we do what we do, the best way to understand Ishmael is to understand the lives of the people who influenced his life. This narrative speaks volumes about African Americans' emotional and spiritual condition.

The narrative begins with Abraham and Sarah being told to leave their kindred and go to the land God will show them. Abraham is told that God will make him a great nation. As a result, at the age of seventy-five, he begins his journey. He is told that he will have an heir from his own loins. Sarah, having borne no children and not trusting God, sends Abraham to her maid Hagar to sire children. Abraham follows Sarah's instructions and takes Hagar as a wife. Hagar conceives and bears a son, whom she names Ishmael (interpreted "God hears") as directed by an angel of the Lord. Before his birth, it is said of him that he will be "a wild ass of a man," against everyone and everyone against him. Sarah does eventually conceive and bears a son, whom they name Isaac. At the time of Isaac's birth, Ishmael is fourteen years of age. When Isaac is weaned, Ishmael is approximately seventeen.

This narrative reveals a great deal about the relational dynamics of women and men that we experience every day within the African American community. Sarah could not have children, so she gave another woman to her husband. This was her decision, her plan; but when her plan was actualized, she became angry. Sarah's initial decision to send Abraham to Hagar's arms was based upon her childlessness. She understood her value as a woman to be directly linked to her ability to bear children. So rather than "lose her man," she did what she thought would please him and secure her desires at the same time.

On the surface, Sarah's actions look really crazy. Yet we could argue that she was behaving within the normal boundaries of her culture. While such an argument would explain her actions, it would place distance between her actions and our own. The fact is that we, men and women, are not very different from Sarah. I recall a situation when I was being propositioned by another woman. This woman was also married. She told me how tired she was of her husband and that she had instructed him to go out and get himself a girlfriend to have sex with because she wasn't interested. Then she proceeded with her proposition of me, which I declined. Her attitude was no different from Sarah's. She was willing to send her husband into the arms of another in order to secure her own desires.

Sarah's and Abraham's actions are good examples of what we believe about adulthood. We live with the pressure of believing that adulthood is the same as parenthood. We have tied adulthood—that is, manhood and womanhood—so closely to procreation that we have come to believe that until we have children, we are not men and women. Anytime womanhood is tied to procreation and there is no child, a woman is prone to becoming like Sarah, who sends Abraham to Hagar. Today a woman does this either through threatening to leave her man, or through an attitude that forces him away, while thinking that her removal from the scene will allow him to have children with another. Many men become like Abraham, following the exact will of Sarah (not that it always takes much to push us). Such a push reinforces the idea in our minds that men must sire children to be "real" men. Some men seek to prove their "manly" worth by having children all over the city or by sleeping with as many women as they can in addition to their wives. Most men have a desire to father children. Children can fulfill the manly needs to be procreative, generative, and immortal.

We have experienced the negative consequences of having tied adulthood so closely to physiology and anatomy. Linking adulthood with parenthood has encouraged a loss of intimacy and a lack of responsibility within our relationships. For many, as long as the world can see that we made a baby, that is all the validation our relationship needs. Personal value is associated with physical performance. "What I do" with my body becomes more important than "who I am" as a person. In fact, what I do tends to be such a strong motivation that who I am really doesn't matter.

The pressures of parenthood can lead to a loss of intimacy in a relationship. Sometimes men and women can barely share themselves in openness and honesty due to a preoccupation with becoming parents. It is important to be clear about your desire for children. Be sure that your desire is out of love and not out of a desire to improve your self-esteem. The couples that desire parenthood for esteem will find their greatest challenge if infertility is an issue. Many never recover from such a blow. Relationships carry a great responsibility.

In some instances, a connection is not made between baby and responsibility. Here, I am thinking beyond the contemporary common critique of "babies having babies." Babies having babies has less to do with a person's age and more to do with a person's attitude. Having children does not make anyone a mature and responsible adult. Youth who have children often say they had the child because they wanted to be loved or have someone to love. Such a motivation is no different from that of older men and women who have a child because they know their self-esteem or social status will improve.

Once Sarah gave birth to Isaac, she tried to undo everything she had done. Ishmael was Abraham's first born son, but after Isaac was born, Sarah moved to eliminate Hagar and Ishmael. The human tendency is to kill what we cannot control. Sarah was unable to control the lives of her husband's second wife and son. Whenever people are unable to live with bad decisions, there is a tendency to remove the physical reminders of those decisions. This is why so many relationships break up so badly. It is easier for people to go away mad than it is for them just to go their separate ways.

We often have a feeling that another must be destroyed if we are to be able to live with our feelings of a bad decision. I have been twice engaged and once married. My first engagement was a real eye-opening experience in many ways. We both knew that if we had gotten married, we would have been miserable, but "neither one of us want[ed] to be the first to say goodbye." Finally, I said I didn't care what she told people. I wanted out. Later, one of the stories I heard from a friend regarding why we broke our engagement was all news to me. The termination of the engagement, according to my ex-fiancée, was due to my unwillingness to commit to her fully. The story she told, although untrue, was one that gave her peace and allowed her to face the world.

One of the prominent arguments among African Americans regarding our identities as men and women has to do with our relationships with our mothers and fathers. I will explore this point at some length in chapter 5, but it is important to begin to consider these issues within the context of our search for home. This is particularly the case since the spiritual foundation of the child tends to be laid by the mother.

When Hagar conceived, she experienced a sense of greater personal worth and value. She was met in the wilderness by an angel of the Lord and told that the fruit of her womb would be extraordinarily blessed. The angel informed her that she would be blessed with a son and he should be called "God Hears," for the Lord had given heed to her afflictions (Genesis 16:11). This experience had a profound influence on the man that Ishmael would become. Hagar's knowledge of having been in the presence of God would influence every interaction she would have with Ishmael. He would be nurtured with a God-consciousness that acknowledged God as very present. She would cling to him as a tangible manifestation of the presence of God in her life. He would be socialized to believe that he was special to the world and that greatness would flow from his being because of God. We could very easily conclude from this that Hagar smothered Ishmael with affection and attention, but it could also be concluded that she was more intentional about growing the boy into a man.

To reflect appropriately on African American female and male spirituality, it is important to note that most of the men of stature in the Bible had close relationships with their mothers. It is the mother who most often initiates the actions that result in divine blessing and nation building in the biblical narratives. While these men of renown are never sniveling weaklings clinging to their mothers, they do start out as "momma's boys." This becomes critical in a social context like African America, in which it is sometimes suggested that mothers emasculate their sons. More importantly, we must consider the dynamic histories of men and women together if we are to have any hope of relational reconciliation. We cannot look just at the men or just at the women. We must consider the reciprocal influence we have had on one another.

Ishmael's story is told primarily through the life of his mother, Hagar. Although Ishmael is a secondary character, God often speaks to Hagar for Ishmael's benefit regarding his future. The first crucial point we need to recognize is that most men come to know God through a connection with their mothers. Today that connection radically affects our ability to find a spiritual church home. Interestingly, the mother-child relationship tends to be transformed into a relationship with the "church-as-mother" later in life. I believe that one of the reasons it takes men so long to dedicate themselves to the life of the church is that we spend most of our lives trying to prove that we are "real men" and not "momma's boys." As a result, there is a developmental phenomenon men engage in behaviors that seek to demonstrate radical separation and difference between mother and son. This is perhaps why there is such a great emphasis on "Father God" and less of an emphasis on "Mother Church." We need to understand, therefore, that real men are connected in intimate ways to mother and sister as well as father and brother.

For centuries, women have taught boys to be men. The mother is the one who lays the primary foundations for identity and personality. Men have been nurtured by mothers, grandmothers, and surrogates. We have learned to understand and interpret the world through their eyes and experiences. We are guided through life by their sensibilities. Our passion and compassion are the result of their nurture. Without losing our male nature, we have matured to become real men. As in Ishmael's case, a woman's experience tends to be a man's first teacher and measure for interpreting life. Our task is not to extinguish that experience from our lives but to integrate it. This also means that women must be extremely careful with how they nurture the male nature. Our survival as men and women need not be dependent upon the destruction of the other in the name of

relational unity. We must break through our segregationist ide-
ologies in order to become more relational in our worldview.
More will be said about this point in chapter 6.

After Isaac was born, Sarah told Abraham that Hagar and
Ishmael had to go! Abraham, in a dutiful manner, told Hagar
and Ishmael that they had to go. To ease his conscience he gave
them a little something for their journey and then sent them on
their way. During this episode, Ishmael lost his name. After
Isaac's emergence, Ishmael and his mother are referred to as
"that slave woman and her son." Prior to this, they were identified by their names, Ishmael and Hagar. Both are objectified
for the purpose of elimination. It is easy to get rid of nonbeings.
When Africans were being sent into American slavery, names
were one of the earliest losses.

Within a patriarchal society, where we are identified by our
fathers and the men in our lives, to have women as one's only
identifiable reference point is degrading. Ishmael lost his home
and his name. Under such circumstances the fight to declare
one's patriarchal rights becomes all important. He and Hagar
were kicked out of the house when Ishmael was approximately
seventeen years old (although the story reads at this point like
he was much younger).

Imagine what Hagar and Ishmael must have felt. They were
abused, used, and denied human dignity. Yes, they were given
their freedom from servitude, but they were not compensated
for the anguish they experienced. Where were their repara-
tions? Hagar and Ishmael did not leave Abraham's household
as respected, free beings. They were sent on their way without
enough food and water to sustain them for an extended length
of time. They were made objects without personal names. With
Hagar and Ishmael out of sight and out of mind, Abraham
and Sarah could live guilt-free. That is the way of segregation,
which is something we know very well as African Americans.

On a family level, consider the number of fathers who have
given up their children in a similar way. Consider the number of
men who have been abandoned by nonsupportive fathers. Consider the number of women who have been discarded after they
had outlived their "usefulness." These actions have led many to

conclude that manhood means abandonment; it means leaving the ones you love or being left. Consequently, many men are wanderers with a profound feeling of rejection. We have difficulty committing to anything or anyone, always feeling that one day those we love will fail us. This is why many men do not settle, settle with great difficulty, or refuse to stay settled.

On the other side, when Daddy is gone, Mommy is left to carry on. Yet, there came a point when even Hagar abandoned Ishmael in the wilderness. Not desiring to see her son die, she leaves him alone to die, in isolation. From their places of isolation, they cry out separately to God; and, as Ishmael's name translates, "God hears" his cry. Our life experiences shape our behaviors and influence our choices. Rather than seeking to give him peace in death, she leaves him with the terror of loneliness in death. Having felt abandoned herself, Hagar found it easy to abandon another.

The pain caused by abandonment takes up residence in Ishmael's being as a fear that he will be abandoned by another, and so he trusts no one and fights to keep everyone at bay, even women. Too many of us live in fear of abandonment. We are so afraid of being left alone that we force ourselves to live in isolation, trusting no one with our hearts. It is no coincidence that Ishmael became an expert with the bow—able to kill effectively from a distance while maintaining personal safety. With the bow he was in control, never allowing anyone to get close to him again. Many of our relationships are similar. Men and women are often a "bowshot" apart—close enough to see one another, yet too far apart to be in an intimate and supportive relationship with one another. We dominate one another with some symbol of power, which is often used as a weapon against the other. Closing this gap will not be achieved by men meeting with men *only* or women meeting with women *only*. I place emphasis on "only" because there is value in meeting separately. But after the separate meetings, there must be a time of togetherness. If our issues include abandonment, meetings in isolation are not the way to heal that pain. Our problems were created both together and apart; the resolutions must include mutuality.

Given all these issues, it should be no surprise that the angel said Ishmael "shall be a wild ass of a man, with his hand against everyone, and everyone's hand against him; and he shall live at odds with all his kin" (Genesis 16:12). Ishmael's socialization taught him that there is no such thing as a home. There was for him truly no place of safety and security. He was always on guard against anyone who might offer familial sanctuary. He was abandoned by father and mother, and all other hands were against him. The desert, where the basic issue is survival, became his dwelling place.

This narrative reveals many issues that are relevant to African America. Our socialization has not changed, and each of us feels abandoned by someone significant in our lives. Communality requires a high degree of interdependence; yet our various separations and segregation have necessitated that African American women and men develop high levels of independence in order to avoid feelings of abandonment. Although collectively we have not lost the hope of unity, our conduct, in many ways, can be interpreted as continuing to function self-defensively. African American women express their defensiveness through emotional aggressiveness and physical "signifying." African American men express their defensiveness through emotional withdrawal and physical aggressiveness. The Spirit says those who have been bruised must be liberated. It is past time for us to be home. We need to be set free from jail and cease from our wanderings. We can find a home if we are willing to open our hearts.

CONSIDERATIONS FOR CARING

- How close can you get to someone and still be comfortable? Are you comfortable shaking hands? Do you shake with one hand or both hands? Are you comfortable hugging everyone? Work on becoming more comfortable with yourself and others.

- What color classification has been given to your body? Where does your color classification locate you socially? What shades of meaning have you given to your skin tone?

- In what ways have you sacrificed your desires to be an equal partner in relationship? What has it cost you to do so?

- How do you participate in degrading men and women?

- Begin to think of your personal body space as sacred. Sharing your space with another makes the relationship a sacred moment. What would it mean to see your relationships as sacred?

- Reinforce communality in your everyday living.

- Choose relational life over the death called racism.

- Develop new relational images that express our identity as a people and our solidarity in relationship.

- Remember that adulthood does not equal parenthood. You have a primary responsibility to be who God has made you to be.

- Talk with someone you trust about the issues you have with regard to abandonment.

Chapter 4

Liberating Our Dignity, Saving Our Souls

*For how can I bear to see the calamity that is coming on
my people? Or how can I bear to see the destruction of
my kindred?* —ESTHER 8:6

What does it mean to be a nurturing community in the face of
painful, isolating oppression? As we consider our history of being forced to separate from those we love, it is important that
we reevaluate our relationships prior to slavocracy. What was
the organizing principle of the African community prior to the
Atlantic slave trade? What are the African communal reten-
tions and extensions that remain as critical resources? African
spirituality is regularly highlighted as an African American saving grace, yet many of the ways in which spirituality seems to
be expressed among African Americans today promotes separation. In this chapter, I explore African American ideas about
community. My main argument pushes for the necessity of
reuniting religiosity and community as essential for restoring
all of our relationships. In addition, I offer a psychospiritual
perspective for our liberation as a people of God.

COMMUNALITY IS THE KEY

One of the basic guiding principles of African life is the idea of
communality. Most Africans think first and foremost in terms
of the good of the group, that is, the community. They sec-
ondly think of themselves, but only as individuals related to
the group. Communality holds everyone, the living and the

ancestors, in proximity to one another. This is, however, a radically different notion from what most Americans understand community to be. In the United States, community is generally understood to be "my neighborhood" or "my church," in other words, my small, individualized community.

For most Americans, community includes only those with whom one chooses to have a relationship and near whom one chooses to live. It is an individualized concept of "me and mine" that is defined through ideas of in-group and out-group cliques and social classes. There are often particular qualifications for community membership according to the U.S. understanding. If you do not live near me and I have no consciousness or positive regard for your presence, then there is nothing communal about our existence. We, in effect, have no relationship. Community, within this narrow understanding, means *my* little group of special friends. It means those who are the same as me in exclusive ways. All are not welcome at this type of community party. The driving force within this framework is an us-against-them mentality. This is completely opposite to the African understanding of the nature of relationship.

African communality acknowledges the interrelatedness of all things and people. Communality is the understanding that all life is interconnected. It sets the tone for seeing and being in the world. The highest community value is cooperation. Although African life has a hierarchical structure, there is a clear interdependence of relationality that extends from the spirit world through the natural world. A communal relationship exists among the supreme being, divinities, and ancestors, who are all a part of the spirit world. The spirit world extends to and includes the communal relationships of human beings, who also have a relationship with all of nature. And we cannot overlook the fact that nature is inhabited by the divine spirits.

Life, in the African worldview, is an intimate and integrated web. In this web of connection all of life is spiritual. One result of this understanding is a special sense of responsibility for the well-being of everyone and everything. There is a recognition that human actions or inactivity have an impact upon all of life, and we are responsible for the maintenance of the connections.

One view of the world holds that human beings are the priests who mediate between the spirit world and nature.

The key features that guide communality are spirituality and responsibility. African spirituality is more than an engagement of spiritual matters like prayer. It is also more than an engagement of the spirit world, like talking to ancestors. African spirituality is the acknowledgment that life is in everything. Moreover, it is not just the acknowledgment but the engagement with *all* aspects of life. African spirituality is a process that integrates all parts of the human self with other selves. It integrates individual and collective lives with all other realms of existence, including nature, humanity, the spirit world, and God's world. Spirituality makes all of one's parts a unified whole, all of one's relationships harmonious and whole, all of one's ritual practices purposefully relational.

Spirituality makes the one many and the many one. Through spirituality, one person is connected to the masses, and the masses are in solidarity. It is the spiritual interconnectedness of all people and all things that situates the individual within the world. One's identity comes from one's connectedness to the community, and without that connection, there is no identifiable being. We know ourselves because we are known by others in the community.

This sense of self, which is a collective sense, makes understandable the statement, "I am because we are; and because we are, I am." An individual life is given meaning only within the context of the life of the whole community. This also means that one's responsibility extends beyond one's self. The individual "me, myself, and I" is substituted with "we and us." According to this view, we are as responsible for the well-being of others as we are for ourselves; and if we do not consider others, we do not care for ourselves. "Love your neighbor as yourself" (Leviticus 19:18) is embedded in African communality.

The spirit world is influential in the occurrences of everyday living. Because human beings are spiritual beings, everything physical has a corresponding spiritual effect. We can do nothing that does not have an impact upon our spiritual life or the spirit world. This also means that all actions affect the individual and the collective at the same time. Poor ways of relating on the social level result in poor ways of relating on the spiritual level. If a person is having family problems, it is generally understood that the extended family, including ancestors, also experiences brokenness. In addition, if we break communion with our ancestors, it is believed that we will experience many hardships in life. Failure to perform special rituals can result in community disaster. We are individually and collectively responsible for everything and everyone.

In the U.S. context, we often operate under the notion that our individual wrongs are okay as long as they do not affect someone else. Within the African context, however, all of our actions, for good or ill, constantly affect others. Broken relationships within this world or between this world and the spirit world affect all of our relationships. Because everything is connected, broken relationships also affect the communal quality of life. Everyone is responsible to and for everyone else who makes up the community. All human beings and living things, including the family, clan, tribe, and nature, are connected. If we damage a part of the community, we damage the whole community.

COMMUNALITY AND VILLAGE LIFE

Because spirituality in Africa is all-encompassing and inclusive, every human event, action, and interaction is sacred. This understanding makes every meeting and activity a sacred event. Standing, walking, working, playing, or resting (alone or with a companion) is always in the presence of the Divine. One is never completely alone because life itself is a spiritual force, and we are always surrounded by the Life Force. In chapter 3, I talked about space relationships. Through the power of word and sound, every meeting is declared to be sacred space, which in turn makes the village holy ground. There is no worship building in African traditional religion. The entire village is a sanctuary. Every village leader has religious and spiritual significance. Every resident of the village is a member of the religious community.

The entire structure of village life is designed to make each person a responsible spiritual being. The central idea for humanity is the spiritual aspect of human nature. To be responsible in the life of the spirit means that one is relationally responsible. Everyone is connected by a web of relationships through a series of parallel constructions of accountability. The household structure is like the larger clan structure, which is like the larger tribal structure, which is like the larger cosmic structure. On all levels, there is a relational accountability. Every person has a responsibility within the different levels and across the levels. From the individual extending right out to the supreme being, there is a sacred exchange and relationship.

The chief has a sacred charge from the Divine and the ancestors to guide the people with spiritual discernment and justice. Within the sacred space of the village, the integrative process of spirituality becomes a daily lived experience. Through the guidance of the chief or priest, rituals are performed for harmonious living. All present are joined together in the sacred process of ending isolation. Through participation in village activities, all parts of the self become an integrated whole with the community and nature and the Divine.

Nothing happens within village life that is not guided by communality. The sacredness of communality motivates a spirit of cooperation so that even work is a relational event. If the village is to build a school, it is not an artisan's activity alone. The entire village participates in the building program. In the preparation of the mortar, there are those who are responsible for toting the water, others for toting the sand, others the cement, others for the mixing, and still others will tote the mixture to the bricklayers. Spirituality is a lived experience, not simply a function of efficiency. It is essentially a way of showing mutual responsibility and accountability.

COMMUNALITY AS AN AFRICAN AMERICAN LIVED EXPERIENCE

With persons of African ancestry, the sacredness of communality has flowed from Africa to America, and communality has been central to the African American worldview. When African Americans speak of community, we tend *not* to talk about our localized neighborhoods. That would be more of an individual or nuclear understanding. When we say "the black community" we tend to refer to African American culture and all black people everywhere in the United States. The term is collective and all-inclusive in the same way we emphasize the extended family rather than the nuclear family. This does not mean that there are no localized identities. There are times when the characteristics of a neighborhood, a city, or even a state are held as superior. Matters of food and sports are the most common illustrations. Yet, when that happens, it is not with the total exclusion of all others. The collective reality of the African American experience remains an implicit part of the communal understanding. We never totally forget that we are connected by a common experience in America.

African American communal life has been a significant force for the survival of African Americans. The basic tenet of communality has promoted our resistance and bolstered our will to survive in the presence of individualizing oppressive forces. Because American culture has promoted individualism, overwhelming forces have sought to isolate us from one another and break our community identity. To our benefit, we have been able to resist many seductive and life-denying forces. For many years, the Delilah of individualism sought to find the source of our Samson strength. If we had submitted to an individualistic understanding of life a century ago, there would not be a culture or a people known as African American today. We have survived because we have believed that unity is strength. More importantly, we have believed unity is life. Due to the fact that our spirituality recognizes all of life as interdependent, we have endured with a sense of clarity that "if I am going to make it, we all must make it." We have known the importance of depending on one another for our physical and psychospiritual needs. One of the clearest expressions of this is seen in the history of the black church. The black church in America has been the guardian of African spirituality. As such, it has been one of the most significant African American institutions. In the African American church, we can see our strong legacy of holding things in common and supporting one another through communality.

OUR RESTORATION

Although we have a legacy of communality, we also have had the experience of individuality. The United States has a dominant stream that encourages individual success. People have believed they could write their own American success story. Images of individual success have formed what we call the "American Dream." Many have devoted their entire lives to the fulfillment of this dream, as though it were their religion. Although a person may not desire to call the American Dream a religion, it has been empowered by Protestant religion to order a person's life. In fact, the "Protestant work ethic" has played a key role in keeping the American Dream alive. Unfortunately, the dream is not attainable for all. The irony of the "Protestant work ethic," which declares that one's hard work will be rewarded, is that it has been lived out by the dominant culture at our expense.

Due to the individualized activities of many capitalists, our labor has been exploited and has turned a great profit. This exploitation led us to rely on one another for survival within this individualizing system. The promoters of the Protestant work ethic in the U.S. sought our destruction while seeking their own salvation. Our survival was mediated by an African "ethic of care." Our enslavement resulted in generations not compensated for their labor. After Reconstruction, we had generations not fairly compensated for their labor. Through it all, caring for one another was far more important than labor. Interestingly enough, labor has been one of the ways to show care for one another by providing for the needs of others. In that regard, we are not strangers to the actions of the "good" Samaritan. We have been the outcast caring for the wounded within our community. An ethic of care is relationship-oriented whereas a work ethic is individually oriented.

The life-giving activities of the black church have taught us the meaning of liberty. Even for those who were born into slavery, liberty was part of the beating of their hearts. Our authority, power, and freedom were experienced in the communal life of the black church. The life of the church represents our past salvation and our future hope. If we are truly going to care for our relationships, we must be true to who we have been and proceed from points known into our future. An important part of being true to who we have been is communality. This means the African American community must be understood as a collective and not just an assortment of isolated individuals within nuclear families. I suggest looking to the black church as one place that expresses our profound understanding of communality.

The African American church not only typifies the spirituality of African Americans; it has also maintained the continuity of the African American community in general. The church has been the place of gathering for worship and social interaction. In times of crisis, the church was the first stop for responding to the situation. The church organized our social and educational activities and was our refuge in the time of trouble. The black church has been representative of the black experience and the catalyst of African American culture. Much of who we are in America can be attributed to our engagement with the dominant culture, but the black church has always been our touchstone. The dominant culture's approach of dividing the sacred and secular was balanced by the black church's approach of allowing for no separation between the sacred and secular. Our spirituality and religiosity had their ultimate expressions within the comprehensive communality of church life.

The leading reason the black church in America embodies communality is that the black church is a reproduction of African village life in America. We always find a way to maintain the things most important in our lives. I observed the truth of this for African America while in Ghana. I was present during a number of village meetings and communal rituals. At every gathering, I was fascinated by the formulaic resemblance of the village meetings to the worship services of the black church in the United States. Without being aware of it, we have maintained the rituals of village life within the life of the church.

Just as the chief, who sometimes was also a priest, sat as the supreme authority within the village, the black preacher has been regarded as the supreme authority of the church and the prime spokesperson of the community. The chief has a queen mother who serves as advisor and social conscience; the pastor/preacher has had his queen mother in the form of a "mother of the church." The chief has his linguist, who is not a translator as much as an interpreter and megaphone of the message from the chief. One speaks to the linguist rather than directly to the chief. At times, the linguist also has the task of affirming the truth spoken by the chief. The chair of the board of deacons often fills the role of the linguist. The chair makes the public pronouncements that reinforce the vision of the pastor through "moments of emphasis" and as the leader of the "amen corner." The chief's elders became the pastor's joint board made up of the deacons and trustees (or stewards). Finally, the people's overall involvement as the community is expressed within the village and church by the call-and-response of the people. We have not only retained African life; we have extended it here in the United States.

AFRICAN AMERICAN SPIRITUALITY AND FAITH HISTORY

Significant dynamics that make us who we are have been retained by the African American church. The church, as the beating heart of our village in America, fostered our survival and nurtured our culture with a living spirituality and faith. Neither our spirituality nor our faith have been limited to a single moment of expression in a one-day-of-the-week experience. Church is not just a Sunday morning experience. Likewise, spirituality and faith have not been limited to the worship hours of Sunday morning; they are both vital parts of what it has meant to be an African American. To describe the spirituality and faith history of African Americans is to articulate central components of African American culture. Spirituality and faith have nurtured the worldview and encouraged the survival skills that have sustained and stabilized dislocated Africans. In 1441, a group of Portuguese landed in West Africa on a trading expedition. Ten Africans from the Guinea coast were shipped to Portugal as a curiosity. We have known global dislocation ever since.

Although assaulted by dehumanizing forces in chattel slavery, Reconstruction, Jim/Jane Crow, and desegregation, our spirituality and faith history have served to ensure our self-understanding as human beings. The hate-filled hurtful ones who stood against us sought to deny us life, liberty, and happiness. Instead of yielding to those life-denying forces, we have maintained the significance of life and celebrated our life together. When everything around us was committed to destroying our communality, our spirituality and faith encouraged us to weave a close community with strong families. Our humanity and dignity were established by our spirituality, our world given reason by our religion, and our commitment to life has been nurtured by our faith. Instead of yielding to the life-denying forces, we formed a compassionate community grounded in the firm belief that God is with us. The biblical narratives of suffering and triumph became our testimony. The divine proclamations of judgment and justice became our hope. We maintained that nothing could separate us from God or one another, even when familial dismemberment was a constant reality.

DIFFERENTIATING SPIRITUALITY, RELIGION, AND FAITH

Spirituality is broader than many assume and less mysterious than many might contend. More specifically, spirituality integrates passion and compassion. Passion is the energy and desire associated with one's physical being. Compassion is the energy and desire associated with one's emotional being. If one kisses one's spouse, for instance, a passionate kiss is often preferable to a "peck" on the lips. But a passionate kiss without any emotional energy is just a lustful kiss. On the other hand, to give someone a kiss of compassion yet not be willing to do something more to change the person's condition is empty. Expressing one without the other can lead to abuse and neglect. Passion and compassion must move as one force.

Spirituality seeks to connect and maintain the connection between all aspects of our living. It is the charismatic stirring within the soul that stimulates and perpetuates our commitment to living wholly holy lives. To be spiritual should not mean that we are disconnected from the world. Spirituality should mean that one is fully engaged in relationships and life. Spirituality leads us to have an active public witness that seeks justice and liberation as well as a vital personal relationship with the Divine. Spirituality is the active integration of our humanity. Through its expression, we cease to function in parts and begin to live up to our potential as whole human beings. Spirituality results in a singularly directed effort to be in communion with God, self, and others. African spirituality additionally understands the world to be filled with spirits, and God's Spirit is an inescapable presence in the world. There is no place we can be where the Spirit of God is absent. There is nothing we can do that the Spirit is not a part of the activity. Because God is in everything and everyone, the most mundane activity is a spiritual activity. This is why African spirituality declares that there is no separation between the sacred and the secular.

The leading confusions between religion and faith have been brought about by their interchangeable usage as though they are the same. There is a relationship between the two, but their distinctiveness needs to be maintained. Religion is humanity's groping to construct and maintain meaning. Its concern is the human condition in general and the condition of a specific context in particular. Religion in the northern states has the same general concerns as religion in the southern states. Yet, because the living conditions in the North differ from the conditions in the South, the religious expressions often differ. Religion has the goal of bringing order and understanding to chaos and confusion. It attempts to create a space that is safe for human existence. Religion develops myths, rituals, and taboos for a people in order to declare the boundaries of earth and heaven and to define human relationships.

While spirituality integrates the human being, religion orders a world that does not embrace, nurture, or care for the frailties of the human being. It is humanity's attempt to establish and maintain what it means to be human. Faith, on the other hand, has to do with the hope and confidence that one places in God from within a particular *religious* tradition. Faith is a statement of what one believes about the religious system in which one participates. Faith is concerned with the performance of the mandates of God that have been communicated through revelation. It also expresses the confidence that one has in the rituals one performs to ensure one's safety and security. Religion orders the world; faith orders one's steps in the world.

BLACK AMERICANS OF AFRICAN OR ENGLISH ANCESTRY?

During the antebellum period of U.S. history, citizenship was directly linked to being white, English, and Christian. Today, although the racist tone has been removed, we refer to the legacy of "White, English, and Christian" by the identifier "White Anglo-Saxon Protestant" (WASP). This identity was the outgrowth of a religious identity being associated with a national identity. The identification of WASP clearly delineated who was "in" from who was "out." The privileges of citizenship were limited to a specific group of people.

During that era, community was based upon separating those who could be a part of the nation from those who could never belong. Who was in or out was determined by aligning skin color with religion and citizenship. Because dark skin was out, citizenship was not a possibility for dark-skinned people. Consequently, we do not talk about being a Black Anglo-Saxon Protestant (BASP); that is, we do not refer to a time when our citizenship was linked to being black English Christians. However, our aspirations for citizenship have sometimes appeared to be a desire to be BASPs. Citizenship and humanity have tended to be defined according to religious experience and one's associations with a past and a homeland. Since citizenship was defined as applying only to the WASP, we were forever excluded from the national community of the United States.

Our aspirations have sometimes resulted in imitation and emulation of what we are not. For instance, I find it interesting to observe *how* we choose to imitate the wealthy. A primary way we represent the wealthy is with a British accent. When we pretend to be rich, we put on the air of being an English aristocrat. One could conclude that we do not have many examples of black wealth so we imitate what we know, that is, white wealth. Perhaps that is why we are so attracted to the wealth of ancient Egypt. Egypt was a wealthy and powerful black African nation. Looking to such a nation can evoke great pride.

Why must we represent wealth with the language of Great Britain? This question has caused me to wonder to what extent our "die-hard" commitment to the King James Version (KJV) of the Bible is connected to our desire to be citizens of the United States? Given the history of white, English, and Christian, I have sometimes wondered whether our commitment to the KJV has more to do with citizenship than it does with piety of faith. I recognize that it was the first Bible for most of us, and therefore difficult to exchange. Yet, we wear more than one style of clothing and eat more than one variety of food. Why shouldn't we read more than one version of the Bible?

Just as religion has been a feature of U.S. national identity, our religious experience as Americans of African ancestry has been a quest for identity. Freedom, human dignity, and citizenship have been dynamic features of our search to discover what it means to be an African in America. The basic rights that we were denied became the formational forces of our self-identification. The African American church helped us to define a place for ourselves that differed from the place the racist system prepared for us.

The black church created a new world of communal belonging as a remnant of the old world. Rather than attempting to squeeze us into a world that we could not fit, the church brought Africa to America. We declared a world made to include our presence as the blessed of God. The rights of citizenship were replaced by the theme of freedom, and the rugged individualism that remains the hallmark of America was regarded as inappropriate for black life. The extended family system, which, again, is directly related to African spirituality, was the standard for relational interaction. Where the racist system marginalized our being by suggesting that we were the most wretched, soulless creatures of creation, we were compelled to allow nothing to separate us from the love of God. African spirituality is a very creative energy; so when the racist system said no, we spiritually found a way to say yes. Take, for example, the idea that Africans were soulless. Our spirituality led us to declare soul in whatever we do. As a result, we have soul food, soul music, and preachers who preach soul-stirring sermons. We sing, "My soul says yes, Lord."

Looking at the life of the black church as a developmental process explains our reactions as an African American community. While its leading value system was African in origin, we still were residents of America and not totally immune to America's influence. The black church, which began as the "invisible church," was very African in its founding expression. I illustrated this point when I discussed the structure of the African American church as the reproduction of village life. While the church continues to express the village, the village has changed over the years.

One of the features of African traditional religion is its adaptable nature. It takes the new experience and integrates it rather than explaining it away. The invisible church emerged during chattel slavery in the antebellum South as an extension of our African roots. As others have said, we did not convert to Christianity; we converted Christianity to ourselves. The invisible church was an expressive combination of African religion and our experiences in America. You will remember that religion organizes the world. It takes the experiences of life and organizes them in meaningful ways. The final result of African religious adaptability was a church that sometimes looked more American than African.

As the invisible church became more visible, it began to resemble mainstream American Christianity. This could have been due to the strong desire to become American citizens. Ultimately, it meant that many of the important features of African religion have been challenged and lost. Our understanding of what it means to be the church today is the most significant change. Our larger sense of communality is no longer lived out within the church. What was whole has been broken into parts. Denominationalism often has more power than it should, considering we are to be "one church with one Lord."

AFRICAN AMERICAN SPIRITUALITY AND THE CHURCH AND COMMUNITY SPLIT

African American spirituality has a legacy of articulating the unity and continuity of all life. Within the African village, there are family rituals and shrines as well as tribal rituals and a village shrine, but all rituals are for the benefit of the entire village. The sacredness of the family shrine extended to the sacredness of the village. Although shrines vary, they are the sacred places for requesting divine intervention. The shrines have been preserved within many African American churches by our understanding of the "prayer closet." The shrines were preserved in homes that had a special spot for the pictures of Jesus and Martin Luther King Jr. and for the Bible.

Since African spirituality holds that all activities are sacred, there is no distinction between the worshiping community and the working community. They were the same community. Therefore, in a historical sense, it is impossible to conceive of a black community in America without the black church. I recognize the diversity of religious experience in African America. There are many groups that have never affiliated with the church. I am of the opinion, however, that the church has been the dominant group within the African American community.

Although suffering has been prominent in our experience, neither our suffering nor our demise was understood as God's will for our lives. We have believed that what God wanted for us, others sought to withhold from us. But we have also believed that God's ultimate judgment would rule in the end. African American spirituality, rooted in African spirituality, promoted our survival through an insistence that we maintain our self-understanding as whole and holy human beings. Whereas we could have developed psychoses that would have fractured the self and separated us from God, our spirituality maintained that there was no separation between blood and nonblood relations, public and private life, physical and spirit world, church and community. All were a part of the same reality. We remained sane and whole holding on to a passion for life and compassion within life.

Our history presents a worldview that holds all life as sacred and singular, not a world split into parts with irreconcilable differences. Western culture has tended to split ideas into two opposing parts. We have experienced this tendency in our lives through the variety of efforts to enforce segregation. This tendency toward splitting has meant the fracturing of people and things into opposites never to be reunited. Once the two sides are established, there are various arguments to support the separation and to keep the two parts forever separated. The civil rights struggle was an effort to end the segregation between one group identified as pure and another group identified as dirty. And there are those who maintain that integration is an impossibility.

One of the leading paradigms of Western culture has been the separation of the sacred and the secular. Unfortunately, African America, as a culture of the West, has also succumbed to this splitting practice of the West. There was a time when it was clearly understood that the church did not simply have its finger on the pulse of the community; rather, the church was the pulsating life-force of the community! Yet somewhere in our history our spirituality transgressed into a segregated worldview by splitting religiosity from social action. It seems we have broken continuity with African spirituality and declared there *is* a separation between the sacred and secular. Delilah discovered our strength in our thick hair of communality and shaved it from our heads.

What was once conceived as a unified whole has been separated into the split personalities of "church" and "community." One of the results of that separation has been a marginalization of the church, which has increased human alienation. The church has traditionally been the place that helped us to find rest from our wandering. In it, we have been able to find home. It has been our place to find acceptance, respect, and family. If the church is pushed to the margins, then the possibility of our finding an end to our wandering is decreased. Human alienation and homelessness are increased if the church remains separate from the community.

The church, which was once the center, has been moved to the periphery of the African American experience. Because the black church has been the leading educational and social institution of the African American community, its life is representative of the community at large. Just as in the village, the lived experience of African Americans has been a religious one. Our concepts of good, evil, and the world of spirits have remained an integral part of what it has meant to be an African in America. Our historic worldview acknowledged that times were hard but God was good—all the time. A favorite text for many African Americans is, "Weeping may endure for a night, but joy comes in the morning" (Psalm 30:5).

Today, however, the church is regarded by many to be ineffectual and out of touch. Our sense of the primacy of God has been distorted. We are strangers to ourselves and estranged from one another. We have appropriated the American separation of church and state, and supported that distortion of spirituality with arguments of the church against the world. Our argument emphasizes being "in the world and not of the world." We have heard it declared that the church should not be involved in politics, or that the church and religion focus on "pie in the sky" rather than daily living. Given the force of this particular separation, it is a short step to the separation of other types of relationships.

Rather than engaging the world through acts of passion and compassion, we have written people off as "throwaways." Separation from those things and people identified as worldly really means "unholy" and "untouchable." Once the center has been shifted, then everything can be deconstructed. The result is that it becomes easier to oppress one another for reasons of color, sex, sexual orientation, gender, or class. The shifting of the church to the margins allows us to oppress anyone on the grounds of keeping worldly things out of the church. This shift also allows us to disregard the church by declaring church folks to be backward.

Historically, violence was an external force confronted by defense and resistance. We believed in the sanctity of all life and saw the sacred in everything and everyone. Our spirituality and religion functioned as one embodied expression of community and church. Our survival was mediated by our belief in the sacredness of life. We were firmly rooted in the principle, "If I am going to make it, we all must make it." Unfortunately, the pervasive violence of our existence is now both an external and an internal reality, and survival of the fittest individual seems to rule.

Within many human beings, there is a need to feel bigger and better than another. Acting upon those feelings means that we will belittle or eliminate someone else. The decision on how to act depends on how one person understands another's usefulness. As long as something or someone serves a purpose in our existence, we go to great lengths to ensure that the thing or person remains present in our lives. However, the moment we feel the thing or person is out of our control, when we feel that he, she, or it is more problematic than useful, we try to destroy that something or someone. We seek to destroy what we perceive to be useless (either church or community) as a way of securing our own positions. Here, the idea of control is most important.

We live in a world that splits relationships into dominant and subordinate. When relationships are defined in this way, the focus is control. Dominating behavior exercises extreme control over another as a way of controlling one's self or one's surroundings. When the subordinate, however, no longer submits, then the subordinate must be destroyed because she or he is out of control. For example, parents sometimes exercise extreme control over their children as a way of controlling household activity. Severe consequences are often imposed if the children do not follow the strict code of conduct. If the consequences prove to be ineffective in controlling household activities, then the parents either break the will of the child or the child gets put out of the house. African Americans experienced this phenomenon during Reconstruction around the turn of the twentieth century. Many European Americans thought of themselves as adults and African Americans as children. White America sensed a great loss of control after it became clear that black Americans were not content with the conditions under which they had been living. As a result, violence against blacks escalated. The message of the profound brutality was be dominated or die. Many did die, quite violently; and many continue to die, quite violently.

Just as America developed into separate and unequal segregated communities, African America has exercised its segregating behaviors by splitting the church and community. The black church and the black community have both claimed to be separate rather than parts of the same whole. Each points to and identifies what is "other" than itself. Without realizing it, we are caught in the cycle of oppression. We have inflicted the same suffering upon ourselves that has been imposed upon us. We have re-created within African America the dividing lines that have separated us from the American whole.

Cycles of oppression create detailed descriptions of otherness. While the African worldview emphasizes an identity process that proclaims, "I am because we are," the process of oppression emphasizes the back side of the statement and declares, "I am because you are not." This phenomenon has escalated into dysfunctional communality. At first, the church was pitted against the community in a simple tug-of-war, but now we are engaging in acts of homicidal aggression because otherness must be destroyed. There is, however, something we have failed to understand about otherness. Otherness is the mirror reflection of ourselves. It tends to be nothing more than an unacceptable perception of who we are. As a result, when we seek to destroy the church or community, we are engaging in suicide because the other is simply the loathsome parts of ourselves. Our acts to eliminate the church or community mean either we find the church or the community or both to be loathsome. Body scarring can be beautiful, or it can be self-mutilation. Graffiti can be art, or it can be desecration. Are we beautifying or destroying ourselves? Our splitting has done more to destroy from within than to create.

No, we are not fire-bombing churches, as was the case in the mid-1990s. That was an attack upon what outsiders perceived to be the stronghold of the black community. The internal destructive activities can be seen in our sectarian denomina-tionalism and our statements on the preferential favor of God for our individual congregations. We can hear the destructive-ness in our condemnation of the community as the lost world that will be judged by God. On the other side, the community sees itself as what is "real." When the community understands itself as separate from the church, it sees itself confronting the harsh realities of black life in ways that the church does not understand. It sees the church as having illusions about life and preferring to escape into Heaven. The community declares the real to be the here-and-now, not a world beyond what we know. The presence of the sacred for the community is social power. It means surviving another day in defiance of the dehu-manizing system that seeks to end our lives. It means living to see another day against all the odds. In the eyes of a community in opposition to the church, the church is a useless substitute for living. To demonstrate its uselessness, it attacks the church verbally and through vandalism.

Although this point has a ring of self-hate theories revis-ited, I am not attributing our behaviors to self-hatred. I am suggesting that separating what is whole into parts, which is *not* rooted within our human beingness, has produced an in-ternal conflict. Because we have not had a clear understanding of what it means to be whole, we have tried to eliminate the part we feel is inappropriate. Too often, we seek to resolve our lack of unity through destructive behaviors. We are destructive not because we hate ourselves but because we no longer know ourselves. Many of our destructive behaviors are an attempt to bring religious order out of our protracted traumatic lives. It is not unusual for people to be totally frustrated with their own behavior and shout, "I hate what I have become!" We are raging against the alien that we have become. That is different from most notions of black self-hate, which emphasize a hatred of black skin and black African physical characteristics. Self-hatred points to issues of shame about what we are. We have skin color issues and we continue to struggle with images of beauty. Here I am emphasizing the guilt we struggle with because of the things we do.

We no longer know ourselves to be a people that believes "if I am to make it, we all must make it." The attitude heard more often is, "I gotta get mine," or "Getting paid!" Since the violence and victimization of men, women, and children have been escalating, our survival depends upon our ability to end the separations caused by our protracted traumatic existence. We accomplish this by rededicating ourselves to life and communality.

We have the very important task of ending the separation of church and community. If we are going to be healthy, whole, and holy, it is imperative that we mend this breach between church and community and reclaim our legacy of African American spirituality. The reintroduction of the split-off personality into the whole will allow us to embrace church and community as a single liberating and salvific force for African America. It will provide us with a complete sense of self and lead us home. To use a different metaphor, the church is being held hostage; and as long as the church is held hostage, the community will remain under siege. The liberation of our people is dependent upon the reunification of church and community.

REUNITING OUR DIGNITY AND SOUL

One biblical narrative that addresses the dynamic issues of our dilemma is the narrative of "The Bronze Serpent" (Numbers 21:4-9). It is a very short and simple narrative filled with symbols and meaning for our liberation and salvation. Just as we have lost a sense of the wholeness of church and community, we have lost the sense that our dignity is connected to our soul. Instead of maintaining dignity as a soul function, we have attributed dignity to external ideas. Dignity is a feeling or attitude of being a very valuable person. No matter what foul thing you say to people with dignity, you cannot make them change their good feeling about themselves. People with dignity are always able to maintain composure because their source of pride is internal. Shifting our source of dignity from internal to external sources has caused us to imitate rather than originate. When people believe that good things can be found only outside themselves, they refuse to look to themselves for goodness, and so they imitate the goodness they believe others to possess. Our imitation has us engaging in a variety of behaviors that are opposed to maintaining the unity of all things.

The Hebrew word for the Book of Numbers means "in the wilderness." It is a narrative record of the journey of the Israelites after their enslavement in Egypt until they reached the land of promise. Their hardships, trials, and responses are described in this narrative. Because Numbers describes what lies between the point of departure and the destination, this is a very appropriate book for reflecting upon the salvation and liberation of African America. During our captivity within the American system of slavery, the Exodus story became our story. God's mighty acts of justice to bring salvation to God's beloved became our hope and testimony. It is, therefore, natural to consider what followed the Exodus as we consider our own story. Furthermore, I find the Bronze Serpent text particularly insightful for helping African Americans reevaluate our condition and see hope for the future.

The text describes a very long journey and how the people became very discouraged along the way. Their memories of the dangers they had been brought through were insignificant in comparison with the current levels of frustration. They began to speak against God and Moses. Their complaint was that they had been brought out of Egypt only to die in the wilderness. They wanted more and better than what they had. Life in Egypt as they remembered it seemed to be far more desirable than life in the wilderness. What they really wanted was to live their lives like the Egyptians. The Lord, deciding not to accept the people's foolish chatter, sent fiery serpents among them, which bit people, and many died. Seeing the error of their ways, they asked Moses to pray for their forgiveness; and Moses prayed for the people.

In turning against God and Moses, the people turned against the sign and symbol of God's ever-present help. How could they really hope to achieve their wants by criticizing those who had been their greatest resource and help? It was God and Moses who stood against the powers of enslavement. It was God and Moses who broke the chains of bondage and led the people to freedom. Their finger pointing was a suicidal act. They injured the relationship. Their protest was an act of spiritual separation. In speaking against God and Moses as they did, they cut themselves off from God, from Moses, and from their true selves.

African Americans have in like manner turned against the sign and symbol of God's ever-present help. A unified church and community stood against the powers of enslavement and inspired us in the struggle for freedom. Later in our history, although we didn't agree on the methods of civil disobedience, we agreed on the time to act. In our separation of church and community, we have made a spiritual separation between God and us and between one another. By separating rather than holding all things in a unified whole, we break our continuity with our past and destroy the village of our communality. We have torn the soul right out of our being. As we say, "God doesn't like ugly," and our separation is very ugly to God. We cannot expect to do such a thing and not suffer the consequences. All of our relationships are suffering.

God answered the people's accusations by sending poisonous serpents among the people. Symbolically, the serpent represents life and death. It represents the enemy, wisdom, cunning, resurrection, healing, and transformation. The serpent symbolically represents the union of opposites. It holds competing ideas together in a unified whole. For the people in the wilderness, it was their destruction *and* their salvation. Its poison was the consequence of their bad attitude, and, once they had repented, its image resulted in their restoration.

In like manner for African Americans, the forces of evil have sought to destroy our dignity by changing our external reality. The things we have known to be life-giving have become soul-isolating. I believe our problems today stem from focusing on individuality and separation rather than communality and wholeness. We still want to "look and live" like the Egyptians who enslaved us. We have desired to be BASPs instead of Africans in America. As a result, we do to ourselves what our oppressors have done to us. Wholeness is the key. The serpent represents the union of opposites. Even if we perceive the church and community to be opposite, we must unify the two.

Our deliverance will come by our reuniting our dignity and soul. We must make the shift from focusing on external affirmations to looking to our internal inspiration. This has happened for many of us. Many of the things that we have come to know as death are now the signs and symbols for our life. Africa, "the dark continent," which once meant backward now signifies the beginning of Western civilization and our hope. Our dark skin, which once meant degradation and death, now means pride and cultural creativity. American slavery, which once meant shame and weakness, now means enduring strength and love for God, neighbor, and self.

SANKOFA: OUR LIBERATION AND SALVATION

Sankofa is the West African Adinkra symbol that means "go back and fetch it." It encourages the retrieval of learning and wisdom from the past. One representation of this symbol is a bird with an egg in its beak, with its head turned back toward its tail feathers. The egg is representative of the essence of life. When sankofa is represented in this way, it is encouraging us to return and restore the source of our life. Sankofa means that our liberation and salvation will emerge from within. It will emerge from the ashes of the past. We will be saved by remembering and nurturing what we have forgotten.

Our restoration requires that we look to our genesis in the African context and to our past accommodations in the American context. Once we have looked back and claimed the foundational essence of our wisdom, which is rooted in our divine encounter, we can discern the struggle of our present and creatively move into the future. We must once again see that there is no separation between the sacred and secular, the church and community, and understand ourselves to be unified, whole, divinely inspired human beings.

Before we can be about the reconciliation of the church and community, we must address the allegations of ineffectualness being directed at the church. The church has been a leader as we have journeyed from being determined by others to self-determination. Unfortunately, our "sure-footedness" is currently being challenged by voices that criticize and degrade the system that has promoted our survival in this land. These voices ridicule the institution that has helped us to establish our identity as African American people. Ironically enough, the assault upon the church is no longer exclusively European American. Our greatest threat now comes from "mis-educated" African Americans. These are the people who look in the mirror and seek to eliminate what they have been taught is valueless. This group *mis*uses vital methodological approaches that lead to their *mis*interpretations and *mis*representations of our survival. This has resulted in their *mis*understanding the spiritual activities that have sustained us in the U.S. They crusade to convince as many as possible that the black church is our undoing rather than a symbol of our strength.

Carter G. Woodson's analysis of Americans of African descent stands as an ironic, less than hopeful, description of our separated condition. In *The Mis-education of the Negro,* Woodson states that many African Americans have been taught to prefer the traditions of the oppressor to our own heritage. Because the ideology of the separation of church and state often degrades religion, many people are more inclined to identify with the community and turn from the church. As I stated earlier, the educational system of village life was directed toward bringing everything and everyone into relational continuity. Unfortunately, much of the educational system that has been experienced by most African Americans has been directed toward dissection while deemphasizing our religious experience.

Moving in the opposite direction, the church has sometimes failed to bring the reconciling word of peace to a suffering community. It has often failed to emphasize that we do not live in a cloister. Church members are community members. We are the neighbors of those who have no relationship with the church. We are the co-workers of those who are not members of the church. Just because we have a different faith stance does not mean that we should not care for the community of which we are all a part. We have, however, preferred to be *in* the community but not *of* the community. We have preferred to be among them but not see them as a part of ourselves.

What we have not realized is that every time we make a loathsome statement about the church or community, we allude to some guilt or shame we feel within ourselves. Guilt has to do with the things we have done. Shame has to do with what we believe of ourselves. Often, they are connected. Sometimes we believe we are caught in cycles of bad behavior because we believe we are bad at the core. Because of the shameful things we believe about ourselves, we find a reason to do the things we should not. The more distance we create within the church and community, the more difficult it becomes for us to be whole, relational human beings. If we are going to be true to our historical self, we must salvage our essence by remaining focused on the fact that not only do we wrestle against principalities, powers, and spiritual wickedness, we also wrestle against flesh and blood—usually our own.

CONSIDERATIONS FOR CARING

- Reflect on the ways everyone and everything are connected. One place to begin is to think of who you are connected to. Then think of who those persons are connected to. Because everyone always connects to another, we are always connected to everyone. And it doesn't stop there. Because we were formed from the dust of the earth, we are connected to the earth and everything that springs from the earth. The connections are limitless!

- Are your attitudes more individual than communal? How life-giving do you believe your attitudes to be?

- The African American church has been the leading institutional source of African American identity. It helped us to make sense of senseless suffering and gave us confidence to walk into the future. Be clear about your religious history and your faith.

- Reflect on the extent to which you have split the church and community into two irreconcilable parts.

- Explore your own issues of shame and guilt related to being African American.

- Think of some ways you can become more active in the life of your religious and local community.

- Actualize sankofa in your own life. Go back and claim one practice from your family history that you have allowed to slip away.

Chapter 5

Nurturing the Extended Family

God sets the lonely in families.
— PSALM 68:6A

We live in a society that promotes individualism and praises individual achievement. We are encouraged to be competitors, and competition means only *one* person can win. Even when teamwork is the key to success, the team concept often succeeds because of one pivotal player around whom the rest of the team is organized. This individual achievement concept has been the dominant way of understanding families in the United States. The ideal has been the nuclear family headed by the father, around whom the other members of the family are organized. Any family structure that does not conform to this design has been considered a weak family with inadequate values.

We are a full generation beyond the Moynihan Report published in 1965, yet we continue to live beneath the shadow of its indictment. Was the Moynihan Report, which declared black families weak, valid? Was Dan Quayle correct when he asserted that our national problem is due to a loss of family values? Is the African American community deteriorating because of a valueless, inadequate nuclear family structure? From the outside looking in, one could very easily conclude that African American families are weak and in need of strong male leadership. This, however, is a gross misrepresentation of the African American family structure. Such a conclusion denies the strength inherent in African American families. Although there are different types of African American families, the dominant organizing family principle has been the extended family system.

AN OVERVIEW OF AFRICAN AMERICAN FAMILIES

A frequent criticism heard among African Americans regarding African American families is that we are not as closely knit as we used to be. There is a strong opinion that our community ties and family relationships are not as tightly woven as they once were. We regularly take a nostalgic look at a time when it seems we had less but our memory suggests that our relationships meant more. Our collective memory produces consistent reflections of neighborhoods functioning as single family units. In that regard, whether we are reporting about a northern or southern community makes no difference. The common story goes something like: "If I was seen doing something I had no business doing, whoever saw it would beat me. And I always knew that I would get another one when I got home because *she* would call and tell my mother." In those days, according to the nostalgic look, the mother didn't get angry at Miss _____ for beating the child who was not her own. The expectation was, in fact, that every Miss _____ was to treat every child as though the child were her own. But the complaint now is that you better not even think about touching another's child.

Discipline, affection, and community solidarity were all tied together by the concept of family. Blood was not the defining characteristic of family. This does not mean that blood ties have not been important. Even Sly, of Sly and the Family Stone, noted in his song "It's a Family Affair" that "blood is thicker than mud." Blood ties have been extremely important. Yet, because our survival has not been dependent upon individual notions of making it, blood and mud have been of equal importance. In African terms, the blood is sacred, and since the sacred is not separate from the mud, that is, the body, then they are of equal importance. The way we have lived this out within the African American community has been to hold everyone as a relative. Whether blood or mud, it is a family affair. Our endearing terms of "mother," "father," "sister," "brother," "aunt," "uncle," and "cousin" have been more than just descriptions of association or titles of respect. They have been the expressions of deep feelings of affection and connection. It has not mattered whether the person has been known to us for all our life or is one we have just met. Dominant family concepts, therefore, have been adoption and extended family.

When these two features have not been recognized or understood by an outsider examining the African American community, an inaccurate picture has been painted about the things we value the most. This is what happened with the Moynihan Report in 1965. Moynihan looked in all the right places, but he misinterpreted many of the things that he observed. Essentially, he made a value judgment about the African American family structure by comparing it to the American family structure he understood to be superior and normal. He saw his work as comparing apples to apples, but there were things he just didn't take into consideration. His comparison was like comparing Winesap apples with Red Delicious apples. They are two different apple families. Most people who bake would not think of using a Red Delicious for baking. Moynihan evaluated an extended family structure as though it were a nuclear family structure. In this evaluation, our families appeared grossly deficient.

To his credit, he considered many of the factors that have negatively influenced the African American family. He noted things like slavery, Reconstruction, and the inequitable economic system that reinforced segregation. He saw these systems as leading social and historical influences that severely damaged African American lives. What was not said was the extent to which his critique was based upon his place of privilege within the society. His analysis did little to challenge the attitudes that created our very painful life situations. He stated that centuries of exploitation had torn the fabric of African American social life. But he said little or nothing about the efforts of eighteenth- and nineteenth-century Americans who did everything they could to prevent Africans from developing families in America. Furthermore, he noted that white American families achieved a high level of stability while black American families were highly unstable and almost nonexistent. Instances of stable black families were those that most resembled the white families he knew best. His analysis was based upon a patriarchal nuclear family system in which Africans were not "permitted" to take part. We have not survived the oppressions of America as a result of our strength as individuals. To the contrary, we have survived because of the strength of our families.

AFRICAN FAMILIES BEFORE SLAVERY IN THE UNITED STATES

To best understand the organizing force behind our family structure, it is necessary to consider the African family structure before we encountered slavery in the United States. I am convinced that we have two problems related to a contemporary assessment of the African American family. One has to do with the ways we interpret the formation and history of our families. The other has to do with the standards used to talk about African American family values.

The first involves what our families should look like. There are many who want to say that there is but one way to be family, and they point to the nuclear system. The second problem involves a belief that black families are incapable of nurturing moral development. Any time there is talk about unstable black families and deteriorating family values, the underlying assumption is that we lack the capacity for relational commitment and are incapable of moral judgment. The conspiracy to destroy our families has had an impact on all of our relationships. If we are to be able to care for our family relationships, we must understand what our families were like before the *Maafa* (Swahili for the great disaster) in the United States.

Again, African spirituality maintains that all things are connected. There is no separation between sacred and secular, animate and inanimate, blood and nonblood relations. Previously I described African spirituality in terms of the village. Now I am going to describe it in terms of the family. In many ways, it is the same description because the family is simply a part of the total make-up of the village. Family life, like village life, is organized around the ideal of respect for the sacredness of life. That is why ancestors are so important. The reverence and remembrance of ancestors represents the family bond that cannot be broken, not even by death.

One of the foundational connections within the African world is the family. Just as the individual has no identity apart from the community, the community is meaningless without the family. Therein lies the basic difference between the African view and the dominant American view. Many Americans view community as a coalition of individuals who have banded together. This is often the understanding of neighborhood action. However, Africans view community as the relational way of being in the world. We are spirit beings who are connected to one another and to the Creator. Because the community is so important, the family is not understood in individual terms. The nuclear family is not what has been emphasized in the African world. The preferred structure of the family is the extended family structure. The extended family structure existed in Africa prior to our enslavement, and it is the extended family structure that took root in African America.

The survival of the family is the highest concern for African people. Without the family, life comes to an end. Our humanity is derived from our connection to the family, the village, and to God. Therefore, without the family, a person ceases to be a human being. Being attentive to the family means that a person is attentive to humanity and the relationality of all life. This dynamic trait can be seen in James Weldon Johnson's "The Creation." In this powerful presentation, we see life being expanded for the purpose of ending loneliness. God is lonely so God expands life by creating everything, including humanity. To be alive is to be in relationship. No one is to be alone, not even God. As a result, God and family have been the foundation of the African understanding of human life.

This view fosters a whole host of values and responsibilities that each person has in seeking the well-being and survival of the family. Every person must be attentive to issues of religion, community, ancestors, leadership, worship and rituals, marriage, parents and children, sexuality, and health. They are all interrelated issues with everyone responsible for one another and all responsible for family. To become irresponsible toward one part automatically results in irresponsibility toward the whole. The intricate web of connection makes everyone morally responsible for the care of the family. Failure to fulfill this responsibility could result in personal illness or community tragedy.

AFRICAN FAMILY VALUES BEFORE SLAVERY IN THE UNITED STATES

African people have developed very sophisticated ideas about sexuality. Contrary to what most have been taught about African culture, there have always been rules to govern sex for the maintenance of social order. African youth were taught to have a healthy understanding of the body, to be physically and emotionally courageous, and to be sexually responsible. We were not running naked through the jungle lying with anyone and everyone. A high moral code of conduct has always been present within the African social fabric. It held certain behaviors, including certain sexual behaviors, to be shameful. Sexuality was a gift to be experienced responsibly. In fact, initiation lessons often included in-depth instruction on sexuality.

Critical to the African understanding of family is marriage. It has been so important that it can be identified as the central sign and obligation of the family system. As an obligation, it has been linked to the understanding of what it means to be a human being. Marriage has not represented the union of individuals for Africans. Spirituality as an ethic of relationship does not even provide for such an understanding. Marriage has represented the union of families. The decision of whom to marry has not been reserved solely for those seeking to be wed. That would make marriage an individual enterprise. The decision has been a family matter guided by family values. It has included the investigation of each family by the other. Marriage extended the family, even before children were a thought in the minds of the newlyweds. In fact, marriage has represented the union of families.

Included in this worldview is the idea that children are an essential part of the marriage union. But again, the focus of marriage was not just making babies. Marriage and children continue to be considered one aspect ensuring the survival of the family. Infertility, therefore, has been regarded as a threat to family safety. Even in American society, infertility is accompanied by a great deal of guilt and shame. In the absence of children, a marriage is rarely thought of as a family.

Within the African perspective, children are a family obligation, and parenthood requires a great deal of responsibility. Parents are responsible for nurturing their children's spiritual lives and fostering a commitment to communality. To do this, a variety of rites and rituals have existed around pregnancy, birth, naming, and child-rearing. Children are constantly being taught their value to the continuity of life. The family and community are involved in every major transition of a child's life. Communality makes everyone responsible for the development of the child. "It takes a whole village to raise a child" has literally been the case. Children are a symbol of family courage and a sign of the desire to live.

AFRICAN FAMILY VALUES DURING SLAVERY IN THE UNITED STATES

Prior to our enslavement in the Americas, we had a long, rich heritage of covenant with the universe and commitment to marriage and family. Removed from the context of community and family, a person had no sense of home, and life ceased to be recognizable as whole. Without a doubt, life was fractured by the Middle Passage, and community and family were the first traumatic casualties. Because community, family, and humanity walked hand-in-hand, to be denied any one of them was painful. To be stripped of all three at once was devastating.

In chapter 3, I talked about the devastating experience of coming to America. I shared a few of my experiences in viewing the horrors of dungeons in Ghana. I also described the brutality that our ancestors suffered in those spaces. Employing the metaphor of home, I explored the loss of home as a symbol of broken relationships. Ultimately, I declared the Maafa experience to be a violation of everything sacred: community, marriage, family, body, religion, and children. The human endowments and privileges that the slavers held sacred for their own lives were not granted to Africans.

One of the tasks of the slavers was to destroy the moral fiber and humanity of their captives. They took great pleasure in their jobs. They were addicted to the violence that can be so intoxicating. They were bent on the devastation of Africa for their own survival. The destruction of the family attacks both morality and humanity at once. That was their mode of conquest. We can see the same tactical atrocities on a similar scale today. Only now it is called "ethnic cleansing." The principle, however, remains the same: If you destroy the family and its value system, you destroy the people.

There were deliberate efforts made by slavers to break the communality of Africans by means of physical and sexual abuse. Men and women were separated. Families, clans, and tribes were separated. Religion, rituals, modesty, and dignity were also assaulted. Everything the slavers could imagine would give meaning to life they attempted to separate from Africans. But life is stronger than death, and we established new ways of being together. God broke the bonds of loneliness and placed us in new families. The slavers' individualistic mind thought that self-preservation meant individual preservation and submission. Because the African mind was not individualistically oriented, self-preservation meant communal and familial preservation and resistance.

In movies, black folks are often portrayed as self-sacrificing. We often laugh at this and say it is the way we are written out of a movie. Yet I also see this as a reflection of the perception others have of us based upon our history. When individualistic minds see us surrender our individualism, they think we have sacrificed the self. But because our self is given meaning and significance through relationship, our surrender is an act of family and community preservation. We have been guided by this lesson: the greatest love is shown by choosing life in relationship.

The African self exists and has meaning only within the context of community and family. If we are isolated, we are like the son known as the prodigal, who separated himself from his father and brother. Away from his family and community, he was lost. His behavior was sign of just how lost he was. But when he "came to himself," he returned home and was restored to his father, family, and position. Whereas the son made a choice to separate himself from home, Africans were forced into isolation by the Middle Passage and chattel slavery. However, our passion for life and compassion in life empowered us to creatively maintain what our captors sought to destroy: family.

We should not idealize our African past: there were issues that prevented us from being totally united on the continent of Africa. But once we were incarcerated and "bound" for America, our collective misery became the catalyst for breaking the barriers that previously separated us. Where language, rituals, and tribe previously kept us from knowing one another, we learned a new common language, established new rituals, and created a new tribe based upon a nonblood extended family structure. Although the essentials of our value system remained intact and strong, they looked a little different.

With their individualistic interpretations our captors concluded that we had no family loyalties. Furthermore, since the outside onlookers attempted to deny us family ties, they assumed we never developed family values. The onlookers' evaluation was based upon an individual/nuclear family structure whereas the family structure of enslaved Africans was an extended structure. Our deep loyalties were to the survival of all. We valued life and love. Care for one another was the guiding ethic, not an individualized work ethic. Although our status as chattel meant that we had no family rights, family remained a central focus after we arrived in the American colonies. Mothers, fathers, and children lived under the constant threat of being separated, and often were separated. This reality only strengthened our resolve to stay together even when apart.

When we quote the verses in Romans that say nothing shall separate us from love, we know of what we speak!

THE SEXUAL HIERARCHY OF THE U.S. SYSTEM OF SLAVERY

Slavery in the United States was undergirded by a sexual hierarchy that was extremely exploitative. White male landowners were on top, and Africans were on the bottom. Legislative and social power was in the hands of the landholders. Privilege and pleasure were the domain of the landholders. They assumed their power to be divinely ordained. They saw controlling the land and subduing Africans as their mission. The laws were established to feed their appetites and theirs alone. Many laws were designed for their protection and not the protection of the masses.

The landholders' moral conduct was governed by a market economy. The expansion of their holdings was far more important than any moral conscience. They took no responsibility for the suffering they caused. This morally irresponsible attitude directly affected their treatment of African men, women, and families. Since money meant success, money also defined the successful family. Family values were blended with market economy values. Model families were those most economically viable and secure. It seems the patriarchal family structure declared model manhood to be the power of sexual exploitation and model womanhood to be silent complicity. These "model citizens" were extremely abusive without any remorse. They prohibited the economic development of African American families and then declared us to be morally inferior. Yet, our inferiority was based upon their definition of the model family and the conditions they created. They simply affirmed and justified their immorality. One of the weaknesses of the Moynihan Report was that it failed to identify the link between family values and market economy values.

Clearly, the patriarchal system of slavery was a white system. What is less clear is whether we should conclude that the African American system was a matriarchy. There are those who argue for and against identifying our family system as a matriarchy. Most of these arguments are based on two understandings: one, that patriarchy is preferable to matriarchy, and two, that manhood requires that the male be the family leader. There is, however, an alternative. During our enslavement, we developed a system that worked for us under the circumstances. I don't think it was either patriarchal or matriarchal. Some African cultures were matriarchal and some were patriarchal. Some traced their genealogies matrilineally and some patrilineally. When this variety of cultures came together in a context that denied us our traditional family values, all these forms were blended into a system more functional than either a patriarchy or matriarchy. It was during Reconstruction that we began to promote a more patriarchal existence because America is patriarchal.

IS THE AFRICAN AMERICAN FAMILY MATRIARCHAL?

As a child nearing my teen years in the late 1960s, I can recall the rumbling that the black family was a matriarchy. Black women were being told they needed to step down from positions of authority in the family so that black men could step up. Although my mother was divorced from my father, matriarchy was not what I had experienced in my home. I had not observed a matriarchy in the homes of either my maternal or paternal grandparents. I also knew two sets of great-grandparents and did not see a matriarchy there. Even beyond my own family, I did not observe matriarchy in my neighborhood or my church. I remember many women asking, "What in the world are they talking about? A matriarchy in the black community?" I think it is possible for us to be blind to our own condition, but I don't believe that the condition identified as matriarchy is the problem.

If the African American family is a matriarchal system, it has been deemed a problem only because it does not look like the family that has been identified as "perfect." It is imperative that we rethink our history for the purpose of preserving our strengths. Having been sidetracked by the question of whether we ought to be patriarchal or matriarchal, we have continued the separation agenda initiated during the Middle Passage. The destruction of families is the destruction of humanity. When we engage in behavior that separates families, we are simultaneously separating family from what it means to be a human being. By doing so, we cease to maintain the ethic of family so central to African spirituality. Also, the American family system is still connected to market economy values. To keep African American families struggling and believing we are deficient benefits someone other than African Americans. If we understand our families to be market driven, we lose sight of the spiritual nature of the family. If we change our family structure for economic gain, we participate in and promote our own exploitation and destruction.

MATRIARCHY AND THE ABSENTEE FATHER

The emasculation of the African American man has long been a concern of the African American community. I described in chapter 3 the systematic emasculation initiated in the Ghanaian coastal dungeons. Full-grown men were referred to as boys. The benefits of a patriarchal society were not extended to enslaved African men. Every effort was made to shape the man into a docile laborer. All this coupled with the landholders' efforts to keep family structures unstable made manhood and fatherhood difficult enterprises at best. This is, in part, why women have been identified as the strength of the African American family.

Fatherhood for enslaved Africans did not bring with it the same authority as it did for the patriarchal landholders. This is another place where I think we have not been making an appropriate comparison. Again, we need to consider enslaved African men in the context of our community. Evaluating fathers within the community of the enslaved with a patriarchal standard naturally would show them to be deficient, even absent. We need to evaluate them according to the spiritual principles that were at work in the community of the enslaved. Remember, spirituality emphasizes the union of blood and nonblood relations. Thus, the identity of fatherhood was not necessarily based upon blood. Fatherhood could have had more to do with a man's community responsibility.

The basic assessment of fatherhood among enslaved Africans has been guided by a patriarchal standard. However, because they were not afforded patriarchal privileges, we should not judge them by those standards. Unfortunately, we have. So the corrective most have offered has been to reshape fatherhood into a patriarchal, individualistic system. This corrective is a total denial of communality. My criticism: Before we reshape the image of fatherhood, we need to know all the contours of its past and present shape.

I was in conversation with a pastor whose ministerial agenda was to reaffirm the men in his congregation. His major focus was that men need to be fathers, and only a man can grow a man. He shared with me that his reason for being so passionate about this agenda was that he grew up surrounded by women and without a father. He recalled his difficulties growing up. He said that he would tell the young mothers in his church that they were doing good jobs, but the boys needed their fathers if they were to become men. After listening to him for a while, I asked him a few questions. "Are you a man?" Of course his answer was yes. "Are you a good man?" Again he answered yes. "If you are a man and a good man, how did you become a good man growing up without a father?" The point I went on to make is that women can raise (and have been raising) men without emasculating them.

When we examine what has been, we discover a sophisticated system for growing boys into men. We have had a well-established system of mentoring boys into manhood and fatherhood. Even when there was no man in the house, men outside the home provided the modeling needed to build a responsible man through the extended family structure. As we evaluate what is and what ought to be, we need to recognize that the African rites of passage included instruction. As a part of a boy's initiation into manhood, he was usually instructed by men other than the father in the home. Those who promote a patriarchal individualistic system are not promoting a system consistent with our past. The making of a man has been a communal responsibility, not an individual one. Without a doubt, fathers in the home are an important part of the family structure. I only raise a caution about promoting a new system at the expense of the system that has sustained us.

NUCLEAR VERSUS EXTENDED FAMILIES

I acknowledge there are different types of African American families. We are nuclear families, extended families, and differing combinations of the two. There is no single family structure that is right. I am simply saying the structure most consistent with cultural history is the extended structure. Since that is the case, it is important that African American families acknowledge the strong family values present before our captivity. We must remain mindful that our family history did not begin in America. We didn't learn to be family only in the twentieth century. In fact, our extended family system, which existed before our captivity, promoted our survival within the hostile environment of slavery. And while our family values may be different from the mainstream, they are not deficient values.

Many practices that originated in Africa and in slave culture remain a part of our African American family functioning. We continue to see sons bringing brides home at the beginning of marriage. Married daughters return home to give birth. We continue to have cousins, nieces, nephews, aunts, uncles, and grandparents all living under the same roof. Sometimes this is temporary and sometimes permanent. Blood relatives and "play" relatives are all bound together as family. These have not been only rural or southern phenomena. These have a part of our living American legacy from north to south and east to west.

I know the extended family system because it has been a part of my personal lived experience. Everything that I have described I have seen in my own family. My mother took in cousins for different lengths of time. I have aunts who have been surrogate mothers for many. I have even experienced what the Africans might identify as a family compound. In our case, the elder of the family would buy a house or two, next to or near the family homestead. Adult children would then move into them with their families. Again, I am not just talking about the rural areas. I grew up in a northern city and this was my city reality. This was normal in my family and in the neighborhoods in which I lived.

THE LEGALITY VERSUS THE SPIRITUALITY OF MARRIAGE

During the slavery period, it was illegal for Africans in America to be married. Holding on to the spiritual value of family and the responsibility to marry, we wed in defiance of the law. We renegotiated our social circumstances to make our lives match our spiritual beliefs. We resisted surrendering our humanity and married in spite of the prohibition against marriage for the enslaved. Marriage was first and foremost a spiritual commitment made by a spiritual people. What marriage represented then is not what it represents now. Today marriage is more a contractual agreement than it is a spiritual obligation. This is another sign of a market economy defining family values.

We have shifted from an understanding of marriage as religious and communal to regarding it as legal and social. I know that people continue to have church weddings. This does not mean, however, that marriage is still held to be sacred. In my experience, most of the ceremonies I presided over were for nonmembers. A church wedding continues to be part of a "picture perfect" wedding day. Spiritual obligation tends to be the furthest thing from the couple's mind. People continue to associate the ceremony with the church although they have separated spirituality from marriage. There are many wedding coordinators who believe they are in charge of the ceremony and can tell the minister how to officiate. Couples will take months to plan a wedding but not think about marriage until after the legal document has been signed.

No one disagrees that the slave system's disrespect for our marriages has had an impact on our understanding of what it means to be couples living in covenant. But the mere fact that we continued to marry in spite of the legal prohibition against forming families suggests there is something else operating today that prevents us from caring for our relationships. We have lost our sense that spirituality is an ethic for relationship. Marriage has mutated into the union of individuals and is no longer the union of families. As a result, instead of seeing divorce as the dissolution of families, we see it as two individuals terminating a legal contract. Whereas we defied the law that prohibited us from marrying, we now defy the law that binds us in marriage. Marriage has become a legal institution of the market economy, and African Americans are reacting in defiance of the legal system. We are now exercising our individual rights as citizens to dissolve contracts.

CHILDREN OBEY

I have grown up with lots of different sayings and ideas about children. Among the most indelible are: children are to be seen and not heard; children are the church of tomorrow; children are a blessing. These sayings offer a great deal of information about what it has meant to be a child. One idea impressed upon me later in life was the important symbolism of the child within the African American community. The birth of a child always signals the parents' transition into adulthood. I recall a pastor announcing to his congregation that one of the church's musicians had just become a father. The new father was described as "one who came to the church two years ago as a boy. Today he becomes a man with the birth of his first child." There I sat—single, childless, and older than the new father—wondering what this pastor thought of me.

The sayings from my youth allude to the discipline and hope associated with childhood. Statements about childhood today often associate childhood with a lack of discipline and hopelessness. Are the children of today a lost generation? It almost seems as though childhood has become synonymous with criminality. Will we be happy only if we can break their wills and force them to obey? I frequently hear statements that children are disobedient to their parents; babies are having babies; we are losing our children to violence. What does it really mean to care for our children in the context of family?

One group analyzes these observations by saying the problem started when we took prayer out of schools. Another group's analysis says we have become "too modern" and our children are raising themselves. Another group suggests that family time has given way to individual activities like television and video games. Another group says the violence of our culture—expressed in television, movies, and music—is consuming our children. In the final analysis, it seems that these groups are saying that our children have not acquired a sense of religious, communal, or family values. The other side of the final analysis is that they *have* acquired a sense of religious, communal, and family values. They are just not the values that previous generations have known. I believe an important part of our hope for the future has to do with reclaiming our past and passing on that legacy as a living testimony. If our children are to overcome the troubles of this world, they must learn to incorporate the valuable lessons of the past into their vision for the future.

Part of reclaiming our past as it relates to children means reviewing our child-rearing practices. One of the child-rearing essentials I think we have lost is the ability to combine affection and with concerns for safety. Instead of being loving and firm, we harden our children in order for them to be able to face the cruelties of the world in which we live. Of course, preparing our children for life's cruel realities is what we have always done. In times past, however, I believe we tempered the lessons regarding safety with affectionate support. Historically we knew that the strength to survive comes from a caring community. Now survival of the fittest is the ethic that guides the behaviors of our children. Strength is an expression of how cold and calculating one can be. Many want to believe that our children are being taught self-defense, whereas we are really teaching them to "strike first." So, in some ways, our children are indeed very obedient to the lessons of survival we are teaching them.

ABRAHAM'S FAMILY

There is a gospel song that plays on the radio that always makes me cringe. It presents a false picture of Abraham's behavior and what his family actually looked like. One of the stanzas says, "Abraham had a son; Isaac was the only one." Well, Isaac may have been the "chosen" one, but he certainly was not the only one! Abraham had two sons. Ishmael was the firstborn. Abraham also had wives.

Let's face it. Most of the great patriarchs of the faith could not have become deacons in the church today. Neither Abraham, Jacob, nor Moses was the husband of one wife. Earlier I talked about the purity issues of African American men, but African Americans generally have perfection issues. Our efforts to create a perfect image often include masking those actions we perceive to be imperfect. Caring for African American marriage and family means, first and foremost, accepting what is. We should not hide our actions to suit some image of perfection we have created. Second, it means working to create what we agree is good for our community. Just as we live in a society with blended families—that is, people are remarrying and the children from previous marriages are joined as one family—we need to be open to changing images.

The African American family structure and struggle parallel the story of Abraham's family structure and struggle. Of course, there is an initial difference. Abraham was separated from his family in Ur by a choice of faith. African Americans were separated from family by force and fate. Considering only the initial separation for the moment, I think the impact was the same in both cases. There was a painful separation from the known and a journey into the unknown. There was the ever-present feeling of pain that arose with the impossibility of returning home and the feeling of fear that always accompanies the walk into an uncertain future. Because Abraham's faith was in constant tension with his fear, not all of his actions were faithful. He did some things that were undoubtedly motivated by fear, which had painful consequences for his family ties.

I find several details of Abraham's life to be inconsistent with the images that we conjure up when we think of a patriarch. On two occasions, Abraham hid behind his wife Sarah. As the patriarch, he did not always protect her the way we assume a patriarchal leader protects his wife and property. When he feared for his own life in Egypt, he told Pharaoh that Sarah was his sister rather than his wife. Pharaoh then took Sarah to be his own wife. And for the safety of her husband, Sarah submitted to Pharaoh. The couple conspired in the same way while they traveled through the land of Gerar. King Abimelech also was given misleading information regarding Abraham and Sarah's relationship. Surprisingly enough, I have never known Sarah's defense of Abraham to result in her being called a matriarch. Yet, she clearly placed herself in harm's way for the safety of her husband. I also have not known these events to cause Abraham to be considered anything less than a patriarch.

During slavery in the United States, African Americans knew this dynamic all too well. Survival frequently meant submitting the kinship bond and body to another. Because Abraham's actions have not resulted in his marriage being considered matriarchal, I feel we should reconsider the way we have explained the history of our relationships. Was Abraham weak, without care for his wife Sarah? I think not. Both Abraham and Sarah were focused on survival. Their actions were directed toward the survival of one another. They both did what they thought they needed to do to survive.

Situations like Abraham's have caused us to feel helpless. We all like to feel in control of our lives and bodies. When we don't have control, we do all we can to claim or regain control. During our enslavement, our survival meant we did things for one another that were not comfortable, but often necessary. Fearful of experiencing that sense of helplessness again, we are overly controlling and mistrustful with one another. Our fear has caused us to overcompensate in our treatment of one another. African American women have acted on behalf of African American men just as Sarah acted on behalf of Abraham. We have not dealt harshly with Sarah because of her protection. Why should we, then, deal harshly with African American women, who also have been protectors?

Just as Abraham did not protect Sarah's honor while in Egypt or Gerar, he also did not constantly rule over her. Abraham frequently submitted, without challenge, to her will. Abraham was rich in possessions, but without children his riches meant little. In hope, Sarah urged Abraham to take Hagar as a wife so that she might become a surrogate for Sarah's barrenness. Abraham submitted. After Hagar conceived, Sarah regretted her decision. Here again, rather than protecting his second wife and unborn child, he submitted to the will of Sarah and declared that she had power over Hagar. Sarah in turn treated Hagar harshly. Abraham stood by in silent complicity, but who criticizes this great patriarch of the faith? Sarah had a lot of power in that relationship, but who condemns her as a matriarch?

This set of issues is very complex. By today's standards, Abraham would be labeled within a variety of derogatory names that would identify him as weak. Derogatory labels could likewise be applied to many enslaved African men. Some men, for example, were used like stud bulls. This abuse left them in isolation and without the privilege of identifying their children as their own. Many more enslaved African women were taken against their wills by landholders. Whether they were impregnated or not, the wives of the landholders frequently battered the already victimized African women.

Today, extraordinary stress is placed upon African Americans with regard to birthing children. The privileges of adulthood come only with the birth of children. Women who are childless, regardless of their status, are frequently labeled as deficient. Men who are childless are seen as weak. Couples that are childless are seen as selfish or abnormal. The different ways of addressing the issue of childlessness often remain unexplored by African American men and women because of the negative labels that must be borne by the couple. This is an area where the silence must be broken. Our relational life depends on it.

As Abraham journeyed, his nephew Lot was included as a part of his household. At the point when Lot's herds became too large, the two went their separate ways. Clearly, the extended family structure was the way Abraham's family life was organized. It was as though Lot was with him just long enough to get himself established, and then he moved on. The same kind of care was an important part of African American migrations from the South to the North in the United States. Northern family members supported their southern relatives until such time as they were financially able to establish their own homes.

If anything, Abraham was consistent in his submission to authority. Ishmael was born; then Sarah bore Isaac. When Sarah chose to have Hagar and Ishmael expelled from the household, Abraham fell in line. The driving issue was the inheritance. The text states that Abraham was distressed but he took no course of action to keep his son Ishmael close to him. Hagar and Ishmael were sent out to die or start life anew. They survived beyond their captivity and established a new family.

During U.S. slavery, we remained classified as chattel until we were liberated from our bondage. Because we were considered immature children in need of our bondage, it was thought that we would die outside of our enslavement. We were sent off with little or nothing. Not even the mulatto children of landholders were considered heirs to their fathers' possessions. We survived, however, and developed strong families. We must not forget our past but build upon it. Looking back can be painful, but we must never forget where we have come from and what we have come through.

Although there is no record that Ishmael ever saw his father alive again, we know that he was present for his father's funeral. He was outcast, but this did not prevent him from showing respect for his past and his father's house. Too many of us want to deny our origins. Without a doubt, our African ancestors played a part in our deportation, which resulted in our exploitation. But just as Ishmael acknowledged Abraham as his father, we must acknowledge Africa as our parent. If we do not claim our past, we will be lost to our future.

Funerals continue to function as impromptu family reunions for African Americans. A funeral is the one event that draws the family insiders together with the family outcasts. Quite often, family fractures are mended by a death in a way life tends not to heal. Maybe that is why death-to-life rituals are so important. They remind us of the importance of being in relationship and the blessing of life. Although funeral rituals are extremely important, we must find new rituals to celebrate life which are not prompted by death.

Finally, considering the events of Abraham's life and his lack of initiative, it seems that father Abraham did not grow his boys into men to become the fathers of nations. Abraham abandoned Ishmael and threatened to sacrifice Isaac. These actions would suggest the lesson to these boys that fathers are not to be trusted. What is clear in these passages is that the mothers guided their boys into manhood. The mothers taught them how to be leaders of the nation. Let us not sacrifice our past systems for the sake of a model that encourages our oppression.

CONSIDERATIONS FOR CARING

- Which is the family structure you are most comfortable with, nuclear or extended? Do you consider your friends to be family?

- The dominant family structure is extended, which is made of blood and nonblood relations.

- Our focus on the family encourages sound moral judgment, relational responsibility, and health.

- Our passion for life and compassion within life reflect our choice to preserve family and community. Our greatest form of resistance has been the choice to love God and others in the face of death.

- When we choose to make decisions about our lives together based upon economics, we are really placing money above our relationship. Be careful not to adopt the immoral attitude of a landholder. The landholders' ideas are not caring; they are criminal.

- Is it necessary for a man to be head of the household to have strong family values?

- Women can grow boys into men without emasculating them.

- Caring for our relationships means accepting what is and working to create what we jointly agree ought to be.

Chapter 6

Transforming African American Manhood and Womanhood

For Adam was first formed, then Eve. And Adam was not deceived, but the woman being deceived was in the transgression.   — I TIMOTHY 2:13–14

I keep a picture of my wife on my desk at the office. During the course of a meeting with a European American woman who was studying with me, she commented that she was glad to see I was married to an African American woman. She had college-age sons, and she said that some of her sons' African American friends dated only white women. She did not disapprove of interracial dating. She just felt that African American women lose out on some of the benefits of life when African American professional men do not marry African American women.

We all have our own attitudes regarding who should be with whom. We look at one couple and say, "They really look good together." But then we look at another couple and say, "I don't know what she sees in him!" We have pictures in our heads of the types of people we believe should be together. We also have differing reactions when the pairings do not match the pictures in our minds. We have reactions at the sight of an African American and a European American together. Many African Americans have heard other African Americans say, "A black woman [or man] can't do anything for me!" How have we become so jaded and mistrustful? Through an exploration of what it means to be men and women, I suggest some reasons why it is so hard to be open and trusting in relationship with one another.

Also included in this exploration is an examination of the concept of evil and how it influences the way we relate. In our relationships, "evil" and "other" are labels we apply to one another when we sense that another has power over us. Because good and evil cannot coexist, we confront evil in an effort to destroy it, thereby making it safe for us to live. Yet what happens when we consider the body evil? Do we seek to destroy our bodies? There is another impulse identified as eros that encourages us to unite with otherness; but because our self-understanding has not been renewed, our unifying efforts are often deceptive.

THE COLOR LINE

American life continues to be greatly influenced by issues of skin color and body type. Together, color and body declare who is acceptable and can belong and who will be rejected and outcast. There are a variety of dividing lines based on color and body. Although we had the notion of an American "melting pot," dividing lines have been more influential in America than the ideal of blending differences.

Establishing dividing lines for separation has been an essential part of U.S. life. The purpose of separation has been to clarify parts and thereby to clarify our relationships. When relationships are founded on separations, mutuality is impossible. If I declare someone to be deficient and designate where she or he belongs, then the nature of our relationship is clearly unequal. The prevailing idea in this perspective on relationship is this: as long as you know your place and stay in your place, we will get along just fine. Relationships that are based on separation ultimately result in one person or group being identified as good and the other person or group as bad. These identifications are often applied to men and women. Depending upon who is observing, both men and women can be good or bad. These are arbitrary attributes assigned to men and women.

They are not congenital, as so many have come to believe. We are taught to identify one person as good and another bad.

This battle of good against evil has been a defining feature of American culture. We have a long history of identifying differences as a way of knowing the enemy. Just as home represents safety, knowing one's enemy helps to maintain personal safety. While the enemy often changes in the course of a person's life, the characteristics of the enemy remain the same. The fight against the enemy is the struggle against evil. In chapter 3, the enemy was described in terms of the African and the black body. I spoke of the influence color has had upon African Americans. We associate colors with feelings, attitudes, and actions that are often described in "black and white." The contrasting colors of white and black are frequently used to identify positive and negative attributes and actions. A good angel is white and a bad angel (or demon) is black. An old southern idiom for doing something right is "do it white." When I was growing up, if a child did something wrong, the threat to "beat the tar out" of the child was often heard. We distinguish lies on a scale on which "white lies" are the least harmful. These contrasts have been adopted by the society at large declaring sacred whiteness as separate from the secular "cold black heart."

BORN INTO THE WORLD

When my oldest godson was growing up, he had the habit of hiding behind doors or around corners until an unsuspecting person would walk by. He would then jump out and shout, "Boo! Did I scare you?" This began fairly early in his life. Not long after he had begun to master language, he tried to scare everyone he could. Our family always understood this practice to be the way his mother "marked" him while he was still in the womb. She has always been a teaser. During her pregnancy, however, she was also quite nervous and easily frightened. We have always believed that her son picked up all this nervous energy. But rather than expressing nervous fear he constantly tried to scare others. And yes, he also enjoys teasing others.

While still in the womb, we are being shaped by the world into which we are born. The developing child learns its first lessons about life from the mother-to-be and from the company the mother-to-be keeps. The developing child responds to the moods, attitudes, and sounds of the external world. The way a child begins to live out life in this world begins while the child is still developing in the womb. Consequently, if the mother is living in turmoil, then the child is born knowing turmoil. If the mother is in a supportive environment, then the child is born knowing something about relationality. Whatever the circumstances of life for the mother-to-be, the newborn begins to interpret and understand life based upon those circumstances.

Every child is affected by the quality of relationships that surround him or her. Think of the attitudes we have about manhood and womanhood. Think about the ways we talk to one another and treat one another. Think about the different ways we treat boys and girls, even as infants. If children born into an environment with low opinions about men or women or family, then they grow up valuing the same things and people that they observed ought to be valued. If children are taught that men are more important than women, then so go the children. If children are taught that individual needs outweigh collective needs, then so go the children. If independence is encouraged and interdependence is ridiculed, then so go the children. We need to carefully examine the messages we give. We can teach a set of nonrelational messages that contradict by our hope to foster close and meaningful relationships.

CHILDHOOD TO ADULTHOOD

We all undergo an educational process in which we are taught what our social roles will be. Each of us has particular ideas about what our responsibilities are as women and men living in the world. Furthermore, these very particular ideas are at the core of how we relate to one another as men and women. Basic to our education is the process of differentiation. We learn to organize our lives around prescribed notions of sameness and difference. We are taught very early in life who is the same

and who is different from us. We learn there are colors for
girls and different colors for boys. We learn there are toys for
boys and different toys for girls. We learn girls are supposed
to cry and boys are not. We learn that boys are to be independent and girls are to be dependent. Our personal needs
are defined through the acts of comparing, contrasting, and
distinguishing our self from other selves.

One of the difficulties we have in noticing this process is due
to the parental statement, "I treat all my children the same."
Naturally, there is a degree to which that is very true. A parent
can love and provide equally. Yet are the provisions for the children the same? Are the children receiving the same treatment
whether they are boys or girls? Are they receiving the same
treatment whether they are fair or dark skinned? While the
old nursery rhyme is no longer spoken, the sentiment remains
the same. Little girls are made of "sugar and spice and everything *nice;*" and little boys are made of "snakes and snails and
puppy dog tails." Among the many messages communicated
by the lines of this rhyme, the idea that girls are nice and boys
are not is quite clear. Also because of our color consciousness,
children are often treated differently based upon skin hue.

A child is constantly bombarded by messages that are at
times contradictory yet have a powerful impact upon the child's
development. There are, in fact, many forces that exert pressure upon our being and encourage us to defend ourselves from
others. These messages are significant as boys and girls grow
into manhood and womanhood. In order to keep from being
overwhelmed by the various messages, every child develops
a filtering system that works as a defense mechanism. This
filtering system helps the child to cope with the pressure of
contradictory messages. It also helps the child avoid total rejection. As a result, our first lessons related to our notions of
manhood and womanhood are received with varying degrees
of resistance.

As I have already suggested, our self-defense mechanisms
are initiated fairly early in life. A toddler engages in a battle
of wills to determine whose "no" will speak the loudest as
the toddler struggles for autonomy. For the toddler to speak

"no" is not an act of aggressive defiance as much as it is an act of self-defense. It is a way of coping with pressure. An act of aggressive defiance would be intended to provoke the parent whereas self-defense is intended to protect the child's sense of rights. The ways we interact with toddlers should cause us to ask this question: Do we desire our children to become emotionally and socially independent, or would we prefer for them to become emotionally and socially dependent? Quite often, the answer depends on whether the child is a boy or a girl. An even larger question is how we appropriately inculturate children into a communal life orientation of interdependence.

Think about our early child-rearing practices. Behaviors we consider to be cute for one sex are considered inappropriate for the other. Protectiveness we believe necessary for one sex is regarded as unnecessary for the other. We often allow boys to get dirtier than girls. We take great delight in declaring children to be little adults: "Mommy's [or Daddy's] little man [or little lady]." These lessons become the primary resources for our self-understanding. They establish the foundation for our areas of responsibility and accountability in relationship. During childhood, the social foundations for our understanding of masculinity and femininity are established. This is the time that our images of womanhood and manhood are impressed upon our minds.

As we physically develop and mature, the struggle for independence is redefined as a struggle for security. I opened chapter 2 by raising the question of when we begin to learn how to negotiate compromises. It is at this time in our development that our self-defense tends to take root as central to negotiating compromises. All our interactions take on a threatening nature, which results in a need to defend our space. We establish spacial barriers to protect ourselves from the world that could do us harm. We distance ourselves from people we have found to be inconsistent. If a parent or teacher shows favoritism while voicing equality, we distance ourselves. Because so much pain has been wrought by the hands of those professing Christianity, many people have chosen to distance themselves from Christianity with its words of love and acts of violence. The KKK, for instance, professes Christian love and despises Africans at the same time.

We find security in predictability to the extent that we know ourselves, we seek the attitudes we know best in the lives of others. To the extent that we can claim a home environment, we seek out or re-create that environment in other places. We tend to function at the level of keeping things the same and moving within what is known. What I am suggesting is that the things we learn at home we seek out in other people and places. That is how we keep ourselves safe, by not venturing far from what we have always known about others. Therein lies an important part of the truth many are fond of proclaiming in the church. A favorite text is Proverbs 22:6, "Train a child in the right way, and when old they will not stray." Here is our early "training." We are taught that men and women behave in particular ways. Our security then becomes dependent upon maintaining those gender distinctions. Self-defense means we close ourselves and hide from others. As a result, sex and gender distinctions become functions of controlling space and individual self-preservation. These ideas affect and influence all of our relationships. For instance, the ideas a man has about manhood as superior affect his ability to work for a woman. These same ideas affect our ability to be friends. This is why the new foundation of openness and trust is so important.

Now think about this within the context of religion and the African American church as it was discussed in chapter 4. The same principles and processes that are active in our religious life have been activated in our relational journey toward knowing what it means to be men and women. Just as we religiously construct a world of safety and security, we religiously ascribe roles to men and women to make our relationships clear and manageable. In fact, our religious convictions often become the primary way of saying, "This is how it is." Historically, it certainly was our way of justifying corporeal punishment within the home. Many of us grew up under the admonishment, "Spare the rod, spoil the child" (Proverbs 13:24). There are many who have known the power of the "switch" (with the three holy leaves at the end) designed to bring home righteousness! My point here is that our religious behaviors have influenced our child-rearing practices and defined the roles we are to fulfill as women and men in community.

WHAT IS EVIL?

The fact that Africans in America are religious people living in an oppressive society means that our worldview is greatly affected by the question of evil. We always want to know how it is that so much evil and suffering can be a part of our existence in the presence of a good God? This is the source of our chanting: "God is good . . . all the time; and all the time . . . God is good." However, implicit in our question of evil and God's goodness is God's location. What is our special relationship to God "when the storms of life are raging"?

Because good and evil belongs to life's eternal struggle, human ideas about God's character and human relationships are often cast in "black and white." In chapter 3, I talked about the struggles we have with our black bodies. Here I am associating the contrasting colors of black and white with the contrasting body types of male and female. We also see men and women as representing good and evil. This is why our black body issues are so complex. White and white bodies have been equated with good; and black and black bodies have been equated with evil. Furthermore, black male bodies have come to represent one kind of evil, and black female bodies have come to represent another kind of evil.

Evil has not been simply the opposite of good; it has been the spiritual force that desires our harm or destruction. This has meant that people have a strong interest in separating themselves from evil and evil-doers. Once evil has been identified as "that one" or "those people," it is a simple matter of avoidance or destruction. Because we, as a people, have been identified as evil, with women and men seen as embodying different types of evil, condemning us has been easy to do. We do stand out in a white crowd. How do African Americans escape from the evil in the world if the evil we see is ourselves? Often this has meant trying to get away from ourselves as dark-skinned men and women. Sometimes it has meant identifying men as evil or women as evil and defending ourselves against one or the other in order to be safe and secure. Considering our relational posture of self-defense, our survival has been understood as our ability to identify, control, and eliminate evil from our lives.

You may recall from chapter 4 my description of the importance of space. The village was experienced as sacred space. Through rituals, both individual and communal, we define our space, making our involvements sacred and distancing ourselves from evil. The old folks used to pray that God would put a "hedge of protection" around loved ones. This was a prayer to keep evil outside the sacred space. We have even seen this symbolized in church. When someone has been filled with the Holy Ghost and shouts or dances, people form a hand-linked circle around the shouting person to keep him or her from physical harm.

Most often, evil is associated with sin or sinners. It is not just a matter of what one does; it is a matter of what one becomes through one's involvement with evil. Purity, holiness, and righteousness become important religious qualities. They help us to define ourselves as good and therefore the opposite of evil. We have tended to understand evil as those events and things outside of the realm and will of God, that is, outside the sacred space. This has resulted in a variety of religious labels that we place on different people. We identify people as "snakes" and "worldly." Women are labeled "Eve" and "Jezebel," both associated with evil.

Another way we have identified evil has been through our understandings of what it means to be men and women in relationship with one another. We confront evil in two ways: (1) by declaring someone to be something totally different from what we are; (2) by renaming someone. When we say that someone is not like us, less than us, or "other" than us, we claim power and privilege over that person. When we are able to give people a name that sticks with them other than a name they desire for themselves, we claim power and privilege over them. We observe these actions in our everyday lives. Both actions have positive usages, but we often use them as our ways of confronting evil. We frequently seek to justify our own sense of goodness by pointing to some evil outside ourselves. We identify someone as other and rename him or her as the embodiment of evil. That evil person is no longer a he or she but becomes an "it." And remember, "It" is always to be avoided in our efforts to get home. But our actions do not stop there. Once someone has been defined as other and named, "It" can be dominated or destroyed.

We can see this clearly with issues related to sexuality. Men and women regularly point at one another describing the other as an evil that can't be avoided, like the fruit in the Garden of Eden. We say things like, "Men [or Women], you can't live with them, and you can't live without them." We don't actually have a love-hate relationship with one another, but we do live in a "push me away–pull me close" style of relating. The women who scream the loudest, "All men are dogs!" are often the ones who enjoy playing "dog-catcher." They will chase a brother until he collapses from exhaustion! The men who scream the loudest, "Women only want what I got!" often work long hours every day to be taken for all they have.

The concept of evil plays an extremely important role in the development of our sexual identities. In chapter 3, I discussed the unhealthy opinions and discomforts we have about our black bodies. I pointed to a history that still lives with us and how we have difficulty being at home with ourselves because of the evil that has been associated with our black bodies. So as we grow from childhood into adulthood and develop a bodily understanding of ourselves, the evil that the larger culture associates with our black bodies becomes our self-understanding. Therefore, the concept of evil greatly affects all of our relationships. No matter what the activity, our maleness and femaleness play important roles in how we relate to one another. No matter whether our relationships are men sharing with men, women sharing with women, or women sharing with men, our understandings of manhood and womanhood influence our interactions.

Just as the church and community have split, men and women have split. We see one as sacred and the other as evil. Because our manhood and womanhood are worked out through our understanding of evil, to identify one's self as good means that self-defense is really protecting the sacred. If good is regarded as manhood or womanhood, then our relationships are a life-and-death struggle of good against evil. Manhood and womanhood are each fighting for the survival of its own goodness against evil. Our actions declare that if goodness is to prevail, then the destruction of evil is absolutely necessary. We see ourselves as winning when we claim our sexual superiority. We believe that good and evil cannot coexist, and so it becomes our sacred duty to control or destroy evil. Establishing one's sexual superiority is seen as the triumph of God in the world. This is one of the basic reasons why we have the battle of the sexes, and why we just can't get along.

We have a host of unstated assumptions about each other that continually shape our relationships. One of the ways I get at these assumptions in my classroom is to ask women the question, "What does it mean to be a man?" and to ask men, "What does it mean to be a woman?" What always comes out in the process is that both men and women have ideas about what they think the other ought to be. We all have been taught what to believe about men and women, and we treat one another according to what we have been taught. Unfortunately, much of what we have been taught has been based upon painful experiences. Those pains have been associated with the evil we believe guides another's behavior. The most disheartening part about the way we relate is that both men and women encourage one another to conform to personal ideas of what we think men and women should be. Once these thoughts are shared by the group, the question that is always asked by both men and women is: How can you believe or expect that of me? While we have an idealized hope for our relationships, the painful experiences of our past often guide the quality of our relationships. It is the same as the learning process we experienced as children. There is an idealized hope combined with a contradictory painful message.

Here is how it works. Women who desire to be in relationship with men have images of the ideal man, but operating beneath that is a message of distrust, such as, "All men are dogs." On the other side, men who desire to be in relationship with women have images of the ideal woman, but operating beneath that is a message of performance, such as, "she just wants what I can do for her." These two points of distrust and performance can be traced back to our dungeon experiences. The two points seem to dominate the relationship even when it is between members of the same sex. Many younger women express distrust of women and therefore prefer the company of men. And many men, driven by competition, measure their male relationships by achievements and possessions. These underlying messages become the guiding principles for conduct with one another. Both messages declare that if I am to be safe as a man or woman, I must never forget this basic truth about the other. As long as I remember this, I can use it to control the relationship. To our detriment, rather than changing the messages and behaviors, we perpetuate them and isolate ourselves from one another. Again, our spirituality of unity and wholeness is reduced to actions of separation.

EROS: OPPOSITES ATTRACT

I was having dinner with some friends one evening enjoying casual conversation, when one person asked me if my wife was the type of person that I thought I would marry. I thought it a rather odd question until I heard my friend's full explanation. She explained that in her experience the ideal person that we have in mind is often different from the person we actually choose. This friend believes we somehow choose a person who is opposite from what we envision as our perfect match. Her opinion puts a little different spin on the idea that opposites attract. In this case, the opposite is the other side of our own ideal of the perfect person for us.

What is it about any of us that finds another attractive? How is it that someone so very different from ourselves can be so attractive? A woman and a man, middle-class and underclass, light skin and dark skin, black and white, rough and gentle, young and old can all be seen as opposites, yet there are perpetual attractions among all of these opposites. Each finds the energy and the will to reach out and embrace the opposite. Sometimes the reaching is true love that overcomes all obstacles. Other times it is a passing fancy to occupy time or satisfy a hunger. In either case, this desire is often described as eros. Eros is a love that reaches for the forbidden and completely opposite. It builds bridges over impassible rivers and valleys. What the world sees as opposite and hateful, eros unifies through passion. In many instances, it is this love that makes two become one.

We are taught fairly early in life to know when someone is the same as us, and how we are to treat what is identified as different. The colors we are dressed in, the toys we are given, the games we play, the differing treatments we receive as boys or girls all make up the lessons we learn early in life. We think there is no problem when baby boys and girls of differing ethnicity play together in their "birthday suits." However, there is an age when they are deemed inappropriate playmates. They are separated and given new messages about difference and warnings about being close. How can we encourage separation for children and then expect to have wholesome, trusting, and open relationships later in life?

Our awareness of sex and gender differences is primarily guided by an educational process. Older siblings, parents, and other adults teach us that some behaviors are appropriate for boys and different behaviors are appropriate for girls. They teach us that we are not alike and the other is to be watched very carefully. We are taught in a variety of ways that men are dishonest and women are cunning and lay traps. It is so ironic that a significant part of what we are taught conditions us to be separate until our sex drive reconditions us to unite. Our sexual reconditioning is what is most often associated with eros. At puberty, the gap of separation that we have been taught must exist is bridged by eros. Unfortunately, separation is still operating as a dominate force in our relationships. The early foundational messages of "stay away" have been so strong that it is virtually impossible for our relationships to begin in trust and openness. Until we learn how to relate in new ways, our relationships will be dishonest responses guided by physical urges. This is also where the split between spirituality and sexuality is most prominent. I said in chapter 4 that spirituality combines passion (physical) and compassion (emotional), and passion without compassion is lust. The result is we dishonestly masquerade our lust as love.

Lust is selfish, motivated by the desire for physical pleasure. Recognizing that selfish behavior is often met by rejection, lust disguises itself in loving gestures. Children learn how to say things in a cute way that will get them what they want. The lines used by a "player" are an adult version of this process. This is often without any concern for the other. Love acts for the purpose of uniting with the other. It desires to share itself with another in an effort to end the isolation. It is the sharing of the self. So many of our efforts, however, are disguises of our true feelings. Lust is not relationship-oriented, which means that caring is improbable. Acts of lust perpetuate separation and isolation. We wear the mask of intimacy for the purpose of individual pleasure.

The lustful tones of our relationships are further complicated by the fact that as we move from childhood into adulthood, we begin to experience the complexities of our black bodies. You will recall that in chapter 3 I talked about the difficulties of being at home in our black bodies. As preadolescents, we are told things about what it means to be African Americans, but they really do not begin to have meaning until we begin to live out our lives through our bodies. It is in our youth, when our hormones are exploding and we are beginning to explore romantic relationships, that we come face-to-face with the messages of the black body and the desire for the other.

Because of the hormonal changes in the body, every young person thinks about physical appearance and physical activity. But all the negative messages about the black body pervert a normal preoccupation with the young body. Rather than facing bodily issues as a normal part of life, we have imposed on us the black bodily issues of hypersexuality, evil, dominance, and power. The direction of our relationships is guided by physical appearance and passion without emotional engagement and compassion. When black body issues guide our behavior, it all comes down to the "booty call." Until we see the false faces we have encouraged and the segregation we promote, healthy relationships and home will continue to be illusive fantasies.

THE GENOCIDE OF RELATIONSHIPS

I know that genocide is a very strong word to associate with relationships, but what else can you call the large-scale destruction of relationships? The Middle Passage, also called the *Maafa,* was a system of genocide. The Middle Passage sought to destroy an entire culture and family system. To destroy a culture is to destroy a people. To destroy a people's family structure is to destroy a people's basis for relationship. Destruction on such a large scale is genocide. By our choosing to continue in these patterns of destructive behavior, we continue the genocide of our relationships.

As we have grown from birth to adulthood, we have had problems understanding the nature of relationships. The relationships of our own choosing are often based upon identifying someone who is "the same as me in every way." We choose someone to be close to because we like the same activities. We have the same opinions. We feel the same about life. Sameness has become the basis for all of our relationships. Even when we talk about opposites attracting, we are still talking about our need for sameness. Sameness, in many ways, minimizes our risks in life. Yet here is the question: Are we the *same* or are we *like* one another?

In the Genesis 1 and 2 creation stories, the following words are recorded: "Then God said, 'Let us make humanity in our image, after our *likeness*'; . . . Then the man said, 'This at last is bone of my bones and flesh of my flesh; she shall be called *Woman,* because she was taken out of *Man.*' " (Genesis 1:26a, 2:23, RSV). Both texts place an emphasis upon "likeness" rather than "sameness." In Genesis 2 the one who "was taken out of man" was given a different name. They were similar but not the same. Although we all have been created in the "likeness" of God, we are not the same as God. While I may be like you in many ways, I am not the same as you.

The problem seems to be that most people are uncomfortable unless things and people are the same. We have been taught there is no unity unless someone is the same as another in every way. A man is not the same as a woman, but there are a number of likenesses that I propose we build upon in order to be more trusting and caring in our relationships. When we hold on to our ideas that everyone must be the same for us to be comfortable and safe, we limit all the variety that God placed in humanity. Also, to live our lives in sameness is to continue to live as victims. Racism and sexism have worked to destroy us in an attempt to uphold an artificial standard of goodness, purity, and dominion. If the standard is white and/or male, then most people are not acceptable. Those who are the same as the standard are the just and saved, and those who do not measure up are the damned. Remember, once we identify someone as other, that is, not the same as me, "It" can be controlled or destroyed.

In the name of sameness and for the sake of unity, we have sacrificially destroyed significant parts of ourselves. Religious people that we are, we believe in sacrifice. Sacrifice is understood as an act to bring peace and end suffering. Also, because we are communally oriented, we believe in self-sacrifice. We believe in doing what is required by the community. Our splitting behaviors and separations, however, have been perverted. As an offering to our sense of superiority, we now sacrifice what we see as less important. If a woman is seen as less important, she is sacrificed. If a man is seen as less important, he is sacrificed. If our children are seen as less important, they are sacrificed. We hear the sacrificial voices saying, "A woman is an evil seductress, sacrifice her. A man is an irresponsible user; sacrifice him. Our children are disobedient and should be seen and not heard; sacrifice them." What we have not recognized is that by destroying the part, we destroy the whole.

We must find a new possibility for mending the split and ending the separation. I am suggesting that a focus upon likeness rather than sameness is one possibility. It is the denial of the likenesses of African American women and men that has caused us to lose sight of the sacredness of our relationships with one another. We no longer see our external appearances and internal spaces as sacred. Therefore, our experiences with one another are rarely experienced as spiritual encounters. Our encounters are too often reduced to a physical event. As an African American man, I am rarely seen or treated as a professional. In fact, I am regularly seen as physically threatening and dangerous. For instance, why is it that each time I travel through a particular international airport I am always selected for a "random" search? In every instance, the only thing conspicuous about me was that I was the only black man at the check-in counter. It does not matter whether I am dressed up or down, the action is still unjust. Furthermore, when we consider that East Indians can be as dark as any on the planet, yet not have the same experiences as other blacks, it comes down to the African who is being held in contempt.

In the historical context of the United States, the African male has not been regarded as a human adult and therefore has never been considered a professional. We have been viewed as boys, beasts, or victimizers at best. Because slavery existed together with white male dominance, there were constant efforts to enforce the idea of black male inferiority. In those instances when inferiority was not emphasized, white fear was heightened by images of the black male as the cunningly dangerous rapist of white women. The result is that we have been denied equal access and opportunities to be responsible providers. We have been demonized, lynched, castrated, and infantilized all in an effort to make us powerless.

Many black males have come to believe that the only way to assert our black manhood is through sexual exploits and violent activities. We live the fantasy of being more endowed and better in bed than other males. Sexual activity continues to operate as our source and symbol of power. To the extent that we have identified money as power, we often used money to reinforce our primary symbol of power, that is, our sexual bodies. The money simply becomes a tool for declaring black male dominance.

On the other side, African women in the system of American slavery were sometimes seen as having more value than men. They were denied the attributes of femininity and required to perform the same labor as men. They were required to increase the slave population through childbearing, and were perceived as more sexually gratifying than other women. Similar ideas exist today in the politics of sex in the workplace. There is a perception that an employer is often inclined to opt for a "two-for-one deal"—a woman and African American rather than an African American man. Whether true or false, these ideas affect the way we relate to one another. They challenge the organization of the household and the survival of the family. If money is seen as the tool for exercising power and dominance, it affects the basis of our trust in relationships. When a woman controls the currency of power in a society governed by male dominance, unless the man is able to understand his manhood in different terms, his relationships are destined for destruction.

Money has been thought to make the woman "manish" or sexless; and the lack of money has been thought to make the man impotent. My wife is a professional who works in an industry where salaries are always higher than those in my chosen career. If I based my manhood on money and earning power, I could never be her husband. Furthermore, if I understood earning power to be a male characteristic, she could never be my wife. Our marriage is not based upon currencies of power, but upon interdependence and mutuality. The only way we will be able to make it is together.

African American sexuality has many layers of problems that negatively influence our spirituality and our relationships. The African American woman is seen as a sex object or a sexless object. The important word here is "object." The male understanding of sex makes her very impersonal, as something to be acted upon rather than someone with whom to be in relationship. The African American man is seen as a sex object and an aggressive animal that is sexually threatening. Our relationships have too often been defined by our physical presence and our body structure. Unfortunately, both the African American man and woman have been affected by the various historical messages of sex and gender that have had painful consequences for our relationships. We battle with eros and spirituality by attracting and repelling one another. These activities make it difficult for us to be at home with anyone.

We continue to live with the old inappropriate ideas that our manhood and womanhood are defined by our reproductive organs and procreation. The gift of procreation has been distorted into personal power and authority. Prowess and procreation have become the defining features of what it means to be African American women and men. Hence, the black woman is seen as a baby-maker or stress reliever. Or she is seen as sexless, as not having a vagina at all, and her value is in her labor and her ability to "home-make." This is a denial of her full womanhood and humanity. Likewise, the black man, who chooses to be known for his bank roll or his bed, reinforces the image that he is a sexual predator. This attitude builds nothing and destroys everything. It is irresponsible and denies his full manhood and humanity. In either case, to live our lives and conduct our relationships according to old stereotypical images developed in the context of slavery is destructive of our humanity.

The slave system sought to destroy African humanity and reduce us to animals to be bred and trained. Why should we want to continue to live such a life-denying existence? If we choose to continue to live this way, we choose to destroy our relationships and our humanity. If we choose to continue to live this way, we align ourselves with evil. And in this case, the destruction of evil is the destruction of ourselves. It is the total and absolute genocide of our humanity.

RELATIONSHIPS AS A HOLY WAR

A guest preacher at my church made a personal statement about the rules for communication between a husband and wife. He informed us that he consults with his wife before any major decision. "I wear the pants in my house," he said. "My wife just tells me which pair to wear." His point was that we all should have relationships that are mutually supportive and respectful. If the relationship is mutual and as she tells him which pants to wear, he should in turn be able to tell her which pants or dress or skirt to wear. This, however, is not the norm for most men and women. Instead of our relationships being guided by interdependence and peace, we make war. Unless we can feel that we have subdued and conquered, we do not feel comfortable in relationship. Throughout this book, I have been examining a variety of reasons why so many of our relationships are uncaring. There is still another influence that affects our relationships as men and women. The way we have interpreted the Bible has also had an impact on our ideas about manhood and womanhood.

African Americans are a people of great faith. Although we continue to be an oral people (that is, we prefer oral traditions to written traditions), we are simultaneously a passionate people of the Book. Yet even as a written resource, the Bible lives as an oral tradition as we retell its stories and proclaim its messages. African American relationships have been shaped not only by our American male-dominated culture, but also by our encounters with the Book.

As a people of the Book, we usually do not interpret statements contained in the Book as the individual opinions of the writers. Although I think we should consider the lives of the writers carefully, I am not trying to suggest that the writers were not divinely inspired. I am however suggesting that sometimes the human condition results in a misrepresentation of what God was inspiring us to say. One of Moses' situations is a good example of this point for me. In Numbers 20:2–13, the wandering Israelites are quarreling with Moses because they are thirsty. Moses and Aaron petition God, and God instructs them to gather everyone together. Moses is to command the rock to give water so that the people can drink. Instead of doing as he is commanded by God, Moses tries to humiliate the people. Then he strikes the rock with his staff. The water comes, but he did not do as he was instructed by God. Moses did it his way, not God's way.

PAUL'S OPINION

There are other instances where I think our way took priority over God's way. Paul's first letter to Timothy 2:8–15 is one of those places where we should seriously consider the possibility that the writer was overly opinionated and not speaking God's way. This text reflects African American attitudes about manhood and womanhood. But I also think this text has less to say about what God has instructed us to believe about manhood and womanhood and more to say about what people have believed. We tend to see this text as instructive of how we are to relate. I see the text, however, as an expression of one man's low opinion of women. Unfortunately, it has been adopted as a "MANdate" from God.

In the course of studying this text, I read it to my wife to hear her reaction to Paul's words. "What he has to say doesn't apply," she said. Women still are not free because of the influence of Paul and texts like this. "That is why I don't like Paul. He believed that men are smarter than women." I also asked her how her grandmother understood this text. She responded that her grandmother saw this text as stating rules of social conduct for how a woman should act in relation to a man. Interestingly, my wife's grandmother was an evangelist who often "spoke" in a family house church. According to my wife's Pentecostal tradition, women don't preach; they speak. Her grandmother also started several churches in her own home. How could she believe she was being led to start a church and still be submissive in matters of church leadership? How are we to understand this text?

This text is not balanced in its claims regarding what a man should do and what a woman should do. Its unevenness actually points to the attitudes that I described earlier, that a woman is considered to be less than a man and evil. The writer manifests a very controlling attitude toward women. Which came first, the text or the attitude? I think the attitude preceded the text; and if we change the attitude, we can have a different understanding of this text.

In this text, Paul describes how a man should worship, but he does not talk about worship for a woman. He says that men are to pray, lifting up holy hands, and then he begins to describe the woman's appearance rather than how she should pray. If we follow this as a prescription, we could conclude that women are not to worship or pray. That would go against the psalmist's understanding that says that everyone who has breath should praise the Lord. In fact, the worshiping congregation in the African American church is predominantly women. If women stopped worshiping and praying, our worship experiences would be far less vital and poorly attended. Why is it that the writer didn't also talk about the way a man should dress and cover himself with good works?

The next issue in the text is the issue of authority. The writer says he permits no woman to teach and thereby have authority over men. She is to keep silent. Silence is not a leading quality for a people with a valuable oral tradition and culture. We know the adage: If speech is silver, silence is golden. Our life experience, however, has been guided by a different sentiment: Silver and gold we have not, but we have a story to tell! Our brothers have talked jive, and our sisters have had sass. Our foreparents have had many "pearls of wisdom" and "mother wit" to share. Through storytelling and folklore, we have claimed our communal authority. This text expresses a social understanding that women are thought to be closer than men to the embodiment of evil. By declaring women evil, men have claimed individual authority and power.

The lack of authority experienced among African American men and women has caused us to act out against one another in unhealthy ways. Our efforts to have control over our lives have resulted in our efforts to control the lives of one another. We have inflicted pain on one another as a way of controlling the pain we feel individually. We control others with the hope of having control over ourselves. For the purpose of pain control, we are homicidal and genocidal toward one another's sexual and gender identities. Our conscious thoughts are not directed toward genocide, but because our activities and reactions are directed toward separation, the result is genocide.

We separate our lives into parts in the name of preserving what is good and noble. Boys are separated from girls. Men are separated from women by defining roles and responsibilities. Rich are separated from poor, so that even if one acquires financial wealth, one is still considered to be less than those with old money. All this separation ultimately ends in the destruction of what it means to be human. Because our separations always results in a hierarchy, separation is never separate and equal. Something always tips the scales. Paul says that men are to pray and women are to clothe themselves modestly. It almost sounds like if men keep their minds off women by praying and women cover themselves so as not to tempt men, then men won't sin. He is saying men are spiritual and women are sexual.

While some of our controlling behaviors are due to pain control, other behaviors are the direct result of an inability to be responsible for our feelings and actions. Although we all should be responsible for our own decisions to act or not to act on sexual impulses, we have preferred to blame one another for having a seductive power over us. Sexual seductive power is never described as good; it is always described as evil. So when African American sexuality is described as evil, it is a battle between white good and black evil. The one who is most often described as being the most sexually seductive is the African American woman.

This epistle seems to speak from the understanding that the woman is a temptress and her seductive power should be controlled. When this understanding becomes the basis of our relationships, we will always be vying for power with one another and wrestling with guilt. Why do I introduce guilt at this point? When spirituality and sexuality are separated, prayer is separate from bodily pleasure. So if there is a longing for physical pleasure, it is thought to be unspiritual and unholy. Such an attitude inhibits prayer life and gives one the feeling of regret for not being more diligent in prayer and holiness. Why can't we see sexuality as a blessed gift? What makes it so difficult for us to see physical expression as an act of prayer? I have a pastor friend who tells the story of another pastor who at the euphoric moment of passion shouts out, "God's good! God's good!" Instead of being overjoyed by the gift, we are overwhelmed by guilt for being tempted. And, of course, it is all "their" fault. "If her dress were longer and not so tight, I would not have lost my prayerful concentration."

The next thing Paul does in this text is to reference the Creation and Fall narratives to support his opinions. This entire text is written in the first person. The writer clearly says "I" and not "God says." After stating his opinion, he attempts to justify it by saying, "Adam was formed first, then Eve; and Adam was not deceived, but the woman was deceived and became a transgressor" (1 Timothy 2:13–14). His starting point is a declaration of superiority: Adam first. And how are we really to understand that Eve was deceived and became a transgressor and not Adam? Without serious thought about this statement, we have allowed all the blame for the human condition to fall to Eve. In that vein, it seems that we sometimes believe that if our marital relationships are going to be successful, the success is dependent upon the woman. Since the story clearly states that both ate the forbidden fruit and became transgressors, to declare that Adam was not deceived means that he made a fully conscious decision to disobey and become a transgressor. The other possibility here is that Paul is saying that Eve made Adam do it, so Adam was innocent. Our judicial system holds that ignorance of the law is no excuse. Furthermore, Adam was not ignorant of God's commandment.

In the pursuit of freedom, authority, and power, women have been made the scapegoats of men. Many African American men believe their underemployment to be the direct result of African American women being more fully employed. There is a feeling that if she is put in her proper place, everything will be made right and perfect. They hold the opinion that women are transgressors because they have stepped out of their roles. These attitudes have not encouraged men to be more responsible in relationships. To the end of making men more responsible, the religious movements that have encouraged men to be more responsive and responsible in relationship are important. My only concern is that we don't elevate one group at the expense of another.

Paul's final words in this text declare that the woman will be saved through childbearing, provided she maintains faith, love, holiness, and modesty. And what of the woman who is faithful, loving, holy, and modest but does not have children? Will she be saved? Is the preaching of the gospel of no effect for the childless woman? I have come to know that infertility is a real issue among couples. There is a tremendous pressure to be married and have children. The assumption today is that if you are married and have no children, you are being selfish. Rarely does the thought occur that childbearing could be a physical impossibility. Is the woman's only value her ability to bear children? Can a man be a man if he has not fathered a child? Is it a man's responsibility to bring salvation to a woman through childbearing? The opinions of this text give us more questions than answers. Its impact upon our lives, however, is unmistakable. These opinions, no matter how questionable, describe and guide our relationships.

ENDING OUR SEPARATION

In our educational systems we separate boys and girls, men and women. It is thought that time apart allows us to develop our sex and gender particularities in order that we might become responsible adults. All too often, however, our separation is more dysfunctional than functional. This happens because we overemphasize certain traits and do not nurture all that we are. The final result is relational hostility and separation. When our first impulse is to be separate, it is difficult for us to be anything other than separate.

"Dysfunctional separation" occurs every time boys are encouraged in their early home education to dissociate from women in order to differentiate. Both men and women have participated in the inappropriate gender education of boys. This has been the male process: Because black male sexuality and the survival of masculinity historically have been paramount, feminine traits have been punishable. Very early we are socialized to begin estranging ourselves from our humanity. We are directed to stamp out behaviors considered feminine. Because the masculine traits that are punishable among girls are encouraged in boys, a boy's first visions of self-worth are often tainted. He often learns that female and feminine are unacceptable. Perhaps this is why so many are so homophobic and misogynistic.

The female process has not been very different. Very early, girls are encouraged to estrange themselves from their humanity by stamping out behaviors considered masculine. They are emotionally abused if they choose to play games other than the relational, noncompetitive games deemed appropriate for little girls. Seeing that the traits that are punishable in boys are encouraged in them, their first visions of self-worth are likewise often tainted. The result has been the sacrificial separation of men from women for the purpose of preserving what is perceived as most valuable. And the next step after separation is annihilation—hence the reprehensible violence of men against women or the devaluing of humanity through acts of lust rather than love.

Each of us must transcend the segregation of the community and the self. Ultimately, we must redefine our notions of manhood and womanhood, our notions of masculinity and femininity if we are to be in relationship and find home. My liberation requires that I maintain relational contact with all the women in my life. This is not just a physical matter; it is also a spiritual one because the oppression of women is the oppression of myself. For, indeed, I am a self that belongs to the people; and isolated from the people, I am a stranger to myself and a destroyer of humanity.

CONSIDERATIONS FOR CARING

- The color line remains an important qualifier with respect to those with whom we will have a relationship. Explore your feelings about to how you came to hold the opinions you do. Which of these feelings have their origin in your childhood?

- If you are a man, answer the question, "What does it mean to be a woman?" If you are a woman, answer the question, "What does it mean to be a man?" Share your answers with other men and women.

- Which have you been taught to value most, dependence, independence, or interdependence? How were those lessons reinforced? Begin to rethink your ideas of manhood and womanhood with an attitude of equality and mutuality.

- Many of our ideas of manhood and womanhood are not structured around mutuality. They are structured around self-defense and individual self-preservation. True manhood and womanhood require openness and trust.

- Do you understand your body to be evil? What is the source of its evil nature? Did God create your body that so many call evil? If God created your body, is your black body evil?

- Reflect on the extent to which your motivations are influenced by distrust and performance. Begin to think about others in new and healthier terms.

- Learn the difference between your loving acts and your lustful acts. Strive to be more loving.

- Focus on likeness rather than sameness. Begin to see your power in your humanity, not in your money. See spirituality and sexuality as a part of both manhood and womanhood.

Chapter 7

Healing Our Brokenness

My joy is gone, grief is upon me.... Is there no balm in Gilead? Is there no physician there? Why then has the health of my poor people not been restored?
—JEREMIAH 8:18A, 22

The first is, "Hear O Israel: the Lord our God, the Lord is one; you shall love the Lord your God with all your heart, and with all your soul, and with all your mind, and with all your strength." The second is this, "You shall love your neighbor as yourself." —MARK 12:29–31

We live with the wounds and bear the scars from generations of brutality and isolation. Although some people like talking about our wounds and scars in terms of redemptive suffering and declare us to be "wounded healers," I am not of that opinion. Too many of us have overidentified with the words found in Isaiah 53 that describe the chosen one as being "wounded for our transgressions... and by his stripes we are healed." We have been wounded *by* the transgressions of others and not *for* the transgressions of others. We are not the saviors of those who violate us. Our suffering is not for their benefit. We are the ones in need of healing. Our redemption and reconciliation are long overdue. The night has been far too long. It is time for morning and joy. I want our grieving over the wounds and scars to come to an end. I want us to be healed through our relationships and be declared "loving healers."

I believe that God intends for life to be joyous. It is supposed to be filled with excitement arising from the new possibilities brought forth with the dawning of a new day. Unfortunately, our struggles are causing us to miss out on the intended abundance of life. Instead of being encouraged to glory in the gift of life, we have been encouraged to "steal, kill, and destroy" love. For generations we have heard, "I punish you because you are unable to take care of yourselves." That was the message of the landholder to the enslaved. We have heard, "I punish you because I love you." That is the message of the parent to the child. We have learned these lessons too well and have come to believe that punishment is the way to show how much we care.

The preservation of our humanity was once a high priority. Although it was difficult to maintain in the face of the inhumane treatment we received, our commitment to life was stronger than death. The combined destructive forces of Cape Coast, the Middle Passage, slavocracy, Reconstruction, segregation, and neoracism declare our history of protracted traumas. Each historical period sought to distort our self-understanding as human beings, but we have been determined to remain human in opposition to the pain. In fact, our entire American experience has been a struggle to maintain human contact. Unfortunately, our acts of preservation have sometimes resulted in negative consequences. There have been times when we did not plan to be hurtful to one another, but we were. Our ability to live together with tender sympathy for one another has been diminished by our fear that another will see our kindness as weakness. Fearful of abuse, we build walls of defense rather than sharing with one another in openness.

We have a grief-stricken past marked by blood, terror, and tears. Yes, we have been terrorized into believing that it is better to use a person than it is to care for one another. We live a protracted traumatic existence as a result of being terrorized for generations. Although individualism is not the foundation of our survival, our relationships have become the survival of the fittest individual. We must not allow individualism to be the basis for our survival in the future. If one person is going to survive, then our entire family and community must survive.

Mutuality is now being avoided by choosing to argue about who is or should be on top. Should the patriarch be on top or should the matriarch? Should a man be over a woman? Should black be over white? We fight to prove that a man can't be a man if a woman is on equal ground. We are more inclined to promote separation than to encourage mutual relationships. We have separated aspects of life that should always remain together. The church from the community, the immediate family from the extended family, men from women are all separations upon which we have based our existence. We spend inordinate amounts of time searching to prove how different we are. We energetically seek to validate our superiority over the other. These separations, in turn, have divided our humanity. If we are truly going to care for our relationships, we must become whole human beings again. If only we would spend as much time working to establish mutuality as we do in working to maintain a system of dominance!

A relational understanding of life acknowledges that our spiritual existence affects our physical existence. It also means that our physical existence affects our spiritual existence. Those areas of our lives that have been fractured need to be integrated and made whole. The main fracture that needs to be mended for healthy relationships is the split that has occurred between our spirituality and our sexuality. This is not a new thought for us, but rather a return to the guiding principles of African spirituality. In order to be whole, we need to be healed.

HEALTH AND HEALING

In earlier chapters, I looked specifically at the ways we split spirituality and sexuality in the contexts of communities, families, and personal relationships. In many of those contexts, the body is frequently identified as bad. If not bad, at the very least, the body tends to be seen as a hindrance to spiritual enlightenment and unity. We have an overwhelming tendency to encourage an absence from the body in order to have a holy experience with the Lord. This condemnation of the body has been conflictive for Africans in America. Historically, we were reduced to a physical people only. Our bodies have been exploited in every way possible: for labor, for sex, for science. Although spirituality has been a resource for our survival, rarely have we been seen as spiritual people.

To our advantage, we also have another understanding of the relationship between spirituality and sexuality that points to the possibility of our healing. When we think of health issues, almost everyone is aware of the intimate relationship between spirit and body. In those instances, many of the negative ideas we have about the body are removed. As a result, good health is understood to be when one is "of sound mind and body," that is, good health requires spirituality and sexuality to be together.

Here are some examples of spirit and body working together for good health. When a spouse dies after many years of marriage, we often suspect that the surviving spouse will soon follow the loved one. When we give up, the body breaks down. We talk about the will to live as essential for overcoming life-threatening diseases. Many recognize the power of prayer for combating illness. Meditation is regarded as a good practice for stress management. Therefore any time we encourage the mind-body split, we encourage the splitting of spirituality and sexuality. When they are kept together, we are fully human and healthier.

Good health is a physical and a spiritual matter. When good health is challenged, healing is required to restore health. An unhealthy body is one that has experienced some sort of breakdown in one or more of the body's systems. An unhealthy spirit is one that has experienced some sort of breakdown in the flow of life energy or the lines of communication between the person, God, and others. If the body is unhealthy, it affects the health of the spirit. If the spirit is unhealthy, it affects the health of the body. Healing restores the body and the spirit to a harmonious relationship. Put simply, healing is the process of being restored to life.

Healing is different from curing. We can find cures for many conditions of the body, but healing the body is a spiritual matter. Healing restores health by transforming the relationship between spirit and body as well as between persons. If an ailment is cured but relationships are not restored, the body's resistance will remain low and may relapse more readily into suffering. I am not denying the importance of the medical profession when I say that healing the body is a spiritual matter. I am simply saying that healing requires more than pharmacology and surgery. Naturally, some physicians would not make the same claim regarding the importance of spirituality to health. There is, however, a growing consciousness among physicians of the importance of spirituality and religion to the healing process.

If we are going to obtain and maintain healthy relationships, we must first be healed. Healthy relationships, like healthy bodies, require a healthy spirituality. Remember, my understanding of spirituality is that it is an integrative process, and like spirituality, healing results in the integration of our being. It makes us whole rather than keeping us separated into parts. Healing restores us to a life of relationships. An unhealthy person feels "less than" and is likely to withdraw from full participation in relationships. Our entire existence in the U.S. has been a fight against the many "less than" messages. Sometimes we have been successful; but the relational problems that we have suggest that we are more often unsuccessful.

There are many different ways the "less than" feeling can express itself and affect our health. Feeling "less than" can encourage self-hate. Self-hate can lead to self-destruction due to an attempt to eliminate the source of the hatred. Much of our "less than" is a condition of shame. This encourages us to hide in despair. As long as we have a feeling of less than, we will never have relationships in which we experience *more than* punishment and pain. Healing transforms relationships and restores us to life. When our wounds are healed, our relationships are open, trusting, and loving.

Throughout this book, I have sought to identify the protracted traumatic stressors of African American people. I have attempted to describe the reasons for our relational struggles with the hope that we will become better equipped to end our traumatized existence. We need to attend to our pain if we are to be healed. We have assumed too many things about the quality of our relationships. First and foremost, we have assumed that we continue to "practice what we have always preached." We assume our relationships to be clear and unified without any separations. But we are living with separations on every level of our existence. Our relationships are not as strong as they need to be. We have not been giving the attentive care needed for healthy relationships.

There are volumes in our popular culture that attempt to say what is real for African American people. If we believe the "hype," we are nothing more than emotional, full of rage, lustful, loud, abusive, violent criminals who are athletically powerful and unintelligent. Furthermore, according to the hype, African American fathers abandon their children, and men are not really men because they have been raised by women. The hype really speaks only to part of our reality. We rely too heavily upon "ideas" of what is, rather than focusing on the "reality" of what we are doing to one another. Our ears are well tuned to hear the negative rhythms and rhymes of abusing and terrorizing one another. How willing are we to work to bring healing and create healthy lives?

The reality of the African American context is that we are spiritual beings who respond to spiritual care. Due to our legacy of pain and suffering in America, we are extremely cautious, even nervous, about allowing someone to be close enough to touch our hearts. We have a long history of the abuse of power, the destruction of our hope, and the devastation of our lives. We live in a society whose contempt for us chained our lives by saying we were crazy outside of slavery, terrorized us "just for the fun of it," experimented on us without our knowledge, and limited our opportunities. Essentially, there has been a blatant disregard for our humanity. It is impossible to live under such pressure and not be affected by it. The place it shows up is in our relationships. We wonder, What does it mean to be faithful to someone? Can I really trust another person to care for me?

We know what it means to be healthy; but in order to achieve good health, we must be healed. If we continue to conduct "business as usual," the end result will be that the wounds of our relationships will go unhealed. We must mend the fracture that exists between our spirituality and our sexuality. Our healing will restore our humanity. It will restore our community. It will restore our families. Our healing will turn men toward women and women toward men. Our healing will turn us into friends and lovers. It will turn the hearts of children toward parents and parents toward children. Our healing will make us whole and holy beings again.

HEALING THROUGH THE RESTORATION OF HUMANITY

The fact that we have not always been acknowledged as human in the United States is undeniable. It was a recorded matter of law that defined Africans as only a fraction of what it means to be human. Even today, our classification as human is sometimes challenged. We are still referred to as animals in the "concrete jungle." The idea that one person can be called human and another person can be called an animal really does beg the question, What does it mean to be human? Before African Americans can be healed through a restoration of our humanity, this question must be answered by the community.

The question of the nature of humanity, although simple, has a very complex answer. Our answer to the question is shaped by our approach to the question. One answer says that human beings are of the genus and species known as Homo sapiens. Humans are the creatures that walk upright, have the power of reasoning, and live according to sophisticated social structures. This answer, however, which largely focuses on behaviors, does not go far enough. It does not address the nature of what it means to be human. The question of "nature" focuses on origins.

The origin of humanity has been the deciding line (or the dividing line) to determine who is human and who is not human. Those persons who have not regarded all people as human have had a type of "Dr. Moreau attitude" about humanity. They have believed that some animals can look like human beings but be different by virtue of their nature. The science-fiction character Dr. Moreau genetically manipulated wild animals in an attempt to make them human in form and behavior. While his genetically altered animals had human characteristics and appearance, they were still regarded as animals. Although they could perform many human functions, they were treated as animals by Moreau.

Those with this "Dr. Moreau attitude" have not considered African Americans to be human beings. They have thought us to be animals imitating humanity. We have been thought to have a separate origin, an animal origin. We have been thought to have a separate nature, an animal nature. By contrast, those who have been considered human have thought of themselves as having a divine origin and nature. Therefore, they have justified their vile treatment of us with the Genesis command to have dominion over the beasts and subdue the earth. They see themselves as obedient to the law of God. Who are "they"? "They" includes anyone who denies the human dignity of another.

In chapter 6, I briefly examined the biblical creation stories. I highlighted how humanity has been created in the image and likeness of God. There we are told that humanity indeed does have a divine origin and nature. I also argued in that chapter that the text emphasizes likeness and not sameness. Just as men and women look at one another and say, "not the same," different people have looked at one another and said, "not the same." In both instances, saying "not the same" has meant that one is human and one is not human. It seems that Africans have always been declared by other people to be on the nonhuman end of the humanity spectrum. This has not been a God determinant. This has been the act of human divisiveness.

There are differences in human existence, but those differences were never intended to name one as human and another as nonhuman. We have used differences to establish dividing lines and set up classifications of superior and inferior. Some of the leading dividing lines are color, sex, gender, and economic viability. All of these lines, discussed in earlier chapters, affect and influence one another and become descriptions and discriminatory qualifications for humanity. If we are to be whole beings, then all of these dividing lines must be erased. We must see all people as the image of the Divine. We must see one another as vessels of the divine Spirit. We are human because we belong to God, God is within us, and we are part of one another.

The African understanding of humanity holds that we have essential parts that make the whole human being. This, of course, is not an African concept exclusively, but the African view shares the concept of humanity having multiple parts. For instance, it is not unusual among Africans to talk about humanity being a combination of body and spirit (soul). My South African brother (by mutual adoption) frequently references this ideal. When he is asked how he is doing, he frequently replies, "Body and soul together." This response comes directly from the African spiritual tradition of no separation. The body is our flesh and blood and the spirit is the life that animates the body, which comes from God. These are African beliefs that blend perfectly with Christian beliefs.

Africans have long believed that some parts of our humanity are from the father, some from the mother, yet all are related to God. This view considers life to be extremely relational. It relates all of our qualities and characteristics in the manner of an extended family. Everyone and everything is related, and the connections ultimately end and begin again with God. Our spirituality leads us to understand our humanity as relational living. Joy comes through our acknowledgment that we are alive. "I am because we are, and because we are I am" a part of the family of God. To live humanly is to live relationally. Our view is consistent with the view of humanity we find presented in Mark's Gospel. We are to love God with *all* our heart, mind, soul, and strength. We are also to love our neighbors as ourselves. As whole beings, we are to love God with all our feelings, thoughts, devotion, and physical strength. And with the totality of our being we cannot participate in self-hate because to do so is to offer hate to our neighbors. As a result, love itself is an action that requires all of our humanity.

In order for us to be healed through the restoration of our humanity, we must bring all the parts that we have split apart back together again. We have been created in the image of God as male and female. That means that the fracture that now exists between men and women must be healed. We are to be whole persons as God is One. We cannot love each other with all of our physical strength (our sexual passion) and ignore all the issues of the heart, mind, and soul (our spiritual compassion). Our sexuality must be in harmony with our spirituality. We cannot continue to regard men as spiritual and women as sexual. Healing restores us to a life where we are sexually responsible and spiritually vulnerable. Each man and woman is a human to be in relationship with, not an object to be controlled. We must be open to experiencing all that life has to offer and open to receiving all that each person has to give.

HEALING THROUGH COMMUNALITY

The dominant culture of the United States is a literary culture oriented around the principle of individuality. What is written is quite often more valuable than what is spoken. As an old advertisement used to say, "Reading is fundamental," but it is also individual. Reading is an activity we do in isolation that allows us to escape into a world all our own. The dominant culture encourages individual activities and individual achievement. Even in the eras when family was stated to be most important, individual freedom and male dominance still controlled the cultural landscape. This cultural approach has the tendency to seek to cure individuals rather than to heal community.

African American culture is an oral culture organized around the principle of communality. Within this context, the story is best experienced in a group context through listening. Also, the experience is not one of just listening quietly to every word; rather it is participatory. It is a communal experience with everyone involved in the story through call-and-response. This is why we have tended to be talkative moviegoers. As an oral people, we do not passively listen to the story; we shout at the characters as though we are a part of the scene. We are active participants as the story is told. This behavior is not intended to be rude; it is oral and communal.

A person has no existence outside of the context of community. There is no life in isolation or individuality. All life is seen through a spiritual interconnectedness, and our whole being is organized around a spirituality of interdependence. Nothing is powerful enough to break community if we nurture our spirituality, not even death. We maintain our communal connection through rituals that even include the community of the ancestors. The problem is we have broken continuity with our spiritual tradition. If we attempt to restore African American relationships from an individual rather than a communal understanding, however, the brokenness we are experiencing will not be healed.

For African Americans to be healed, we must restore God as a member of the family and the community. We can ill afford to see God as a distant relative. Since our humanity is inclusive of being in relationship with God, our health requires that we love our God who is Mother to the motherless, Father to the fatherless, closer than any brother or sister, and friend to the friendless. God is the first Ancestor with whom we are to be connected. Our healing requires that we be reconciled with God. Many who recognize this truth attempt to encourage our restoration through guilt. Guilt cannot be the primary motivation for healing. Actions motivated by guilt often result in resentment once the guilt feelings have subsided.

We have been deceived into believing two untruths related to community: (1) every person is all alone in the world; (2) trust in God is a mental deficiency. While we recognize that we are not alone in the world, we have yet to come to terms with whether we ought to have a relationship with God. We have been taught to trust no one; depend only on yourself and what you can see. "Look out for number one." "Get it before someone else does." America has emphasized individuality as the only source of survival and dependability. This is epitomized by the common adage, "Pull *yourself* up by *your own* bootstraps." We must once again see that those problems characterized as individual have community solutions. To have an individual problem means that one has been separated from the collective. African Americans have problems when we split off from the community and God. The ideal should not be "your own bootstraps" but to "lift as we climb."

Healing through community means that our in-group/out-group splits are ended. We are restored to a life that sees all persons as a part of the whole, whether they desire to be included or not. They may choose not to be included, but their decision will not be the result of our excluding them. Because health is a collective and communal phenomenon, I am related to everything that contains life, and there is life all around me. From this perspective, it is not just a matter of God's activity that makes life sacred; it is a matter of human activity, which is inseparable from God, that makes life sacred.

THE HEALING BALM

Since healing includes spiritual processes, I greatly appreciate the words of the prophet Jeremiah concerning health. Jeremiah lived during a time when health, healthcare, and healing were considered priestly matters. Health was directly related to spirituality and social behavior. Although his calling was to become a prophet, Jeremiah was of the priestly tribe, the Levites. He was the son of a priest and therefore was well acquainted with the priesthood and priestly functions. Jeremiah's prophetic role was clear. He was to shake the spiritual foundation of the people in order to bring about a new physical reality for their lives. His role before the people was not a comfortable one. His calling required him to speak the truth, no matter how unfavorable. In Jeremiah 8:18–22, we hear his diagnosis of what he saw in the lives of his people, and what he saw grieved his heart.

As he walked through his community of the nation of Israel, he observed the despair of the people. They were experiencing great suffering and pain resulting from their feeling that they had been separated from God. This feeling was accompanied by a sense that they were "less than" what they had believed themselves to be as a holy nation. As long as they believed themselves to be with God and believed that God was for them, they had the feeling that no one could stand against them. But here they were feeling abandoned by God. They were living in despair.

Despair can be described as a feeling of being isolated and destitute. Despair sucks all the meaning and joy out of life. It brings a loss of intentionality because despairing persons believe that nothing good can come from them and that there is nothing they can do to change this. Despairing persons believe that the world is not better for their living, and it will not be any worse for their dying. Despair is believing that no one cares, not even God. Despair means living in hopeless isolation.

There is no greater suffering than the suffering that comes from believing that we have been totally abandoned. Their despairing outlook was shaped by their memory of what life used to be like. They were a united and prosperous kingdom, but all that had changed. During the time of this text, the people were probably experiencing a drought. Even with an irrigation system, without rain, plant life withers and dies. Given their understanding of the connection between the physical world and the spiritual world, they believed their spirits were also in need of refreshment. The broken relationship and despair they were experiencing meant there was no growth. Their physical and spiritual droughts had destroyed their joy, caused fear and grief, and diminished their humanity. Jeremiah was observing a very unhealthy people.

In this text, I see Jeremiah crying out with the same despairing hopelessness of the people. It is understandable, however, why he cried with a despairing voice. Jeremiah is an Israelite walking among Israelites. To look at the suffering of his people meant he was looking at his own suffering. He had a compassionate heart for his people. He declared his grief to be beyond healing and his heart sick. He was suffering as he considered the suffering of his people. Jeremiah declared, "When my people are not well, I am not well." The pain of the wound was so deep, it was as though healing was impossible. His heart was broken because of the broken relationship.

In other words, Jeremiah was bearing witness to the interdependent nature of community. One person's condition affects the condition of another because everyone and everything is connected. Health and wellness, therefore, are dependent upon everyone's well-being. If it does not go well for my people, and it does not go well for me, then it also does not go well for the rest of humanity. Everyone has experienced this in various ways. A small-scale example is the person who is very miserable and is determined to make everyone he or she comes in contact with equally miserable. If I can't be happy, no one can be happy! In this understanding, if any part of the community suffers, we all suffer. To some degree, that is why it becomes necessary for some to declare who is in the community and who is out. If I can see you as other than myself, then your existence and suffering don't affect my life. This is, in part, how the African American church and community split has been maintained. When the suffering is considered to have no part with "my" community, my health is assured because everyone in "my" church or community is happy and doing well.

The prophet was witnessing the hard times of his people. As he looked around, he wondered what would restore them to health. "The signs and the sounds of the struggles and sufferings of my people are everywhere I look," he says. "Even if I choose to be unsympathetic regarding their pain, I cannot overlook it. Our pain is so pronounced, I must ask, have we been abandoned by the Lord? Have we been left to stand alone against the powers of evil? They provoke me to anger and then tell me I am being overly sensitive. The times of celebration and thanksgiving are no more, and the days of easy living have gone. I am wounded, even broken, because my people are wounded and broken. Isn't there someone or something to bring relief and healing to the suffering of my people? And if your answer is yes, then why have we not been healed? Why hasn't our health been restored?"

Of course there were doctors in Jeremiah's day, but his point was that the suffering of the people was as much a spiritual problem as it was a physical one. In order for the people to be healed, their relationships with God and one another had to be restored. I have been arguing throughout this book that the healing ingredients are openness, vulnerability, and trust in all of our relationships. The application of this particular balm requires a reexamination of what we say we believe. Then we must become more honest and caring with those relationships we say we value. We have broken relationship with our past, which has resulted in many of the pains we presently experience. If we are to be healed, we must understand our physical sufferings to be part of our spiritual reality. Our relationships are unhealthy because we have broken the intimate relationship between spirituality and sexuality.

HEALING THE BROKENNESS

As human beings, African Americans are spiritual and religious beings. While others may start with a more scientific or philosophical way of describing human nature, we experience our humanity through relationship with God and one another. In an effort to keep us from knowing ourselves as human beings, our relationships were forcibly broken at every level possible. Every good relationship that one can imagine was attacked and broken: our culture, home life, religion, marriages, and families. If living as a human means living in relationship, then broken relationships constitute ultimate suffering. We need to heal our brokenness and be restored to life.

Although we have been assaulted mercilessly by dehumanizing forces within the American context, our spirituality and faith history have encouraged our self-understanding as human beings. Our circumstances during our enslavement were horrible enough to make us "wanna holler," curse God, and die. Yet our spirituality maintained a remnant who believed nothing could separate us from the love of God or keep us from loving one another. Our humanity and dignity were established by our spirituality, our world given reason by our religion, and our commitment to life nurtured by our faith. Our spirituality compelled us to "fight on" knowing everything will be all right. We declared that message in spirituals and hymns saying, "Soon, we will be done with the troubles of this world." "We shall be free and get home someday."

African American spirituality promoted our survival through generations of hard times. We experienced our spirituality as a multilayered, communal understanding of life that brought unity. Our spirituality and faith insisted that we maintain our self-understanding as whole and holy human beings. Our passion and compassion insisted that life is relational and directed our living to be in communion with God and others. This is our history, our legacy, our inheritance. However, we have departed from that dynamic understanding in too many ways. We have broken covenant with our past and with one another. Our lack of trust and fear have negatively influenced our relationships. Our brokenness needs to be healed in order that we might truly find home with one another.

Focusing on our brokenness, someone could conclude that Africans in America are without dignity and beyond redemption. That conclusion is wrong. We should recognize that our brokenness is a condition of circumstance and not a feature of our nature. Our black bodies are not a curse from God. Our hearts are broken, not our black bodies. If we hold that brokenness is our nature, then we become a people without hope and beyond the resources of healing. It should not be concluded that we are flawed people because we are broken. We are broken because our relationships have been flawed. Our openness is undermined by fear. We are afraid to trust because life has taught so many of us that trust brings pain. Yet without trusting one another, our relationships will remain flawed. Our life as human beings will remain less than fulfilling. Our flawed relationships can be corrected if we allow ourselves to trust one another enough to be vulnerable. We can be made perfect through loving.

The New Testament letter of First John lets us know that if we are vulnerable, we can reach perfection. We tend to think of vulnerability only in terms of the hurt we might experience. However, without vulnerability, we experience no growth. Vulnerability means that our defenses are down, which allows for something new. As long as we are defensive, we prevent others from coming near to us. Even if they are bringing good things, defensiveness makes us refuse the gift of another. It is true that we can be hurt if we are vulnerable; but it is equally true that we will not feel joy until we are. "There is no fear in love;

perfect love casts our fear" (1 John 4:18). Such a love requires our all, which includes our spirituality and our sexuality, to heal our brokenness and be restored to health.

The intimate connection of spirituality and sexuality links us to God and one another. With this connection African American health, healing, and wholeness are possible; and with God, all things are possible. We simply need to revive the truth of our former understandings. The restoration of our belief in the interdependence of all things and the power of the community will facilitate our healing and restore our health by making us whole. There is no life in isolation, and healing will come only through caring for our relationships.

CONSIDERATIONS FOR CARING

- Remove the idea of punishment from acts of love as an important part of caring.

- Devote yourself to working to establish a ground for mutuality.

- The splitting of spirituality and sexuality have caused our relationships to be unhealthy. Heal this brokenness to mend relationships and restore life.

- Be healed by claiming your humanity. Each man and woman is a human to be in relationship with, not an object to be controlled.

- Be healed by claiming your place in the community. Be reconciled with God, self, and others. Let us "lift as we climb."

- Broken relationships constitute ultimate suffering. Rely on interdependence to help facilitate healing and restore health.

Notes

1. This book addresses persons of faith within the Christian faith community who seek to improve their relationships. Although my primary audience is the African American Christian community, I am concerned about the quality of life within all racial-ethnic faith communities, but find that addressing this concern would make for a much larger book. Also beyond the scope of this book is the complex issue of African American gays and lesbians. Yet my hope is that gay and lesbian persons will find value here. African American gays and lesbians are equally influenced and affected by our social location and identity as Africans in America. Because I focus on the foundations and quality of all our relationships as African Americans, no African American person is excluded.

2. African American pastoral psychology is interested in the liberation of African Americans. It focuses on African American life in particular and is attentive to African and African American culture, spirituality, religion, and faith. African American pastoral psychology is rooted in human beingness, in somebodiness, rather than the functional, reductionist end that characterizes other approaches to psychology. Therefore, pastoral psychological concerns that are not rooted in the particularities of African America tend to approach African American life from a position of human deficiency. At the very least, a generalized pastoral psychology does not consider the full extent of the trauma of African American people. To say that African American pastoral psychology is "rooted" in human beingness means the approach is alive, dynamic, and life-giving and that it emphasizes communality. African American pastoral psychology not only seeks to improve our quality of life, it also seeks to restore our relationships and to launch a counterattack against the evil that assaults our lives.

3. The purpose of the modification from post-traumatic to protracted-traumatic is to emphasize the mental and emotional traumas associated with being black in America. A traumatic event is defined as an event outside the normal range of human experience. It is one that would be markedly distressing to almost anyone. We have declared for generations that our suffering is outside the "normal range" but, in the words of Isaiah, "Who has believed our report?"

Selected Bibliography

Akbar, Na'im. *Breaking the Chains of Psychological Slavery.* Tallahassee, Fla.: Mind Productions and Associates, 1996.

Bannerman-Richter, Gabriel. *The Practice of Witchcraft in Ghana.* Elk Grove, Calif.: Gabari Publishing Company, 1982.

Ephirim-Donkor, Anthony. *African Spirituality: On Becoming Ancestor.* Trenton, N.J.: Africa World Press, 1997.

Fausto-Sterling, Anne. *Myths of Gender: Biological Theories about Women and Men.* New York: Basic Books, 1985.

Grant, Jacquelyn. *White Women's Christ and Black Women's Jesus: Feminist Christology and Womanist Response.* Atlanta: Scholars Press, 1989.

Hare, Nathan, and Julia Hare. *Crisis in Black Sexual Politics.* San Francisco: Black Think Tank, 1989.

Herskovits, Melville. *The Myth of the Negro Past.* Boston: Beacon Press, 1958.

Hilliard, Asa G. *The Maroon within Us.* Baltimore: Black Classic Press, 1995.

hooks, bell. *Ain't I a Woman.* Boston: South End Press, 1981.

Howe, Leroy T. *The Image of God: A Theology for Pastoral Care and Counseling.* Nashville: Abingdon Press, 1995.

Johnson, James Weldon. *God's Trombones.* 1912. Reprint. New York: Viking Press, 1969.

Jordan, Winthrop. *The White Man's Burden: Historical Origins of Racism in the United States.* New York: Oxford University Press, 1974.

Kelsey, George. *Racism and the Christian Understanding of Man.* New York: Charles Scribner's Sons, 1965.

Kovel, Joel. *White Racism: A Psychohistory.* New York: Columbia University Press, 1984.

Lewis, Diane K. "A Response to Inequality: Black Women, Racism, and Sexism." In *Black Women in America: Social Science Perspectives,* ed. Micheline Malson, Elisabeth Mudimbe-Boyi, Jean O'Barr, and Mary Wyer. Chicago: University of Chicago Press, 1988.

Magesa, Laurenti. *African Religion: The Moral Traditions of Abundant Life.* Maryknoll, N.Y.: Orbis Books, 1997.

Oduyoye, Mercy Amba. *Daughters of Anowa: African Women and Patriarchy.* Maryknoll, N.Y.: Orbis Books, 1995.

Opoku, Kofi Asare. *West African Traditional Religion.* Accra, Ghana: International Private Limited, 1978.

Smith, Theophus H. *Conjuring Culture: Biblical Formations of Black America.* New York: Oxford University Press, 1994.

Weems, Renita. *Just a Sister Away: A Womanist Vision of Women's Relationships in the Bible.* San Diego: LuraMedia, 1988.

White, Joseph L., and Thomas A. Parham. *The Psychology of Blacks: An African American Perspective.* 2d ed. Upper Saddle River, N.J.: Prentice-Hall, 1990.

Williams, Delores. *Sisters in the Wilderness.* Maryknoll, N.Y.: Orbis Books, 1993.

Wimberly, Edward. *African American Pastoral Care.* Nashville: Abingdon Press, 1991.

Woodson, Carter G. *The Mis-Education of the Negro.* Trenton, N.J.: Africa World Press, 1990.